From the Limb of a Grapefruit Tree

A Woman's True-Life Adventure of Self-Reliance and Determination

by
Tina Hurn

DORRANCE
PUBLISHING CO
EST. 1920
PITTSBURGH, PENNSYLVANIA 15238

The contents of this work, including, but not limited to, the accuracy of events, people, and places depicted; opinions expressed; permission to use previously published materials included; and any advice given or actions advocated are solely the responsibility of the author, who assumes all liability for said work and indemnifies the publisher against any claims stemming from publication of the work.

Dorrance Publishing Co
585 Alpha Drive
Pittsburgh, PA 15238
Visit our website at *www.dorrancebookstore.com*

ISBN: 978-1-4809-1992-1
eISBN: 978-1-4809-2107-8

From the Limb of a Grapefruit Tree

A Woman's True-Life Adventure
of Self-Reliance and Determination

CHAPTER ONE
Farm Life

Our family lived on a small farm in Alabama. Eight of us made up the Miller clan, my grandparents, my mom and dad, my dad's bachelor brother Lowell, my sisters, baby Gail, middle sister Carol and me, Tina. We all lived together in a large old farmhouse way outside of the country town of Laverne. I didn't learn until later that we didn't own the land. We lived and worked on it. We were very poor cotton sharecroppers, but my sisters and I didn't realize it. We always had plenty to eat and warm beds in which to sleep, made cozy by granny's homemade quilts.

No-one worked on the Sabbath, so we could hardly wait to get home from church for the food and fun. The women spent most of Saturday preparing the Sunday meal. We usually had a big pot of chicken and dumplings or maybe a baked ham from the smokehouse. Along with that came yarns, home-grown vegetables, cornbread and biscuits with home-churned butter and honey straight from the beehives. In the pir chest was a southern favorite, lane cake; buttery vanilla cake with caramel topping. Workweeks were hard, so everyone had a Sunday nap after which Grandpa would get out his fiddle and Uncle Lowell his guitar. Dad would always sing. After a lively afternoon of music we would have a light supper and Dad would churn ice cream, adding whatever fruit was in season. Dad has a little ritual; to see who would get to lick the ice cream paddle. With a twinkle in his eye, he would let us draw straws. He always own, until one of us finally noticed he was secretly breaking his straw in half. In those days dad was one of our heroes. We were living a wonderful life, at least through a child's eyes.

My earliest memory of turmoil was at age four and as life proceeded, I wondered if that would always continue to be the case. I recall standing beside my mom, grandma and grandpa, hugging the legs of my dad and Uncle Lowell. My sisters and I were sad and crying not really understanding where they were going and why they were leaving. The most devastating war in recorded history had broken out over central Europe on September 1st, 1939. German armies began pouring across the Polish borders from the north, south and west. World War II had begun. This seems to me, looking back, as the beginning of the end of my childhood. The most important men in our lives were leaving and we didn't know when, or if, they would return. German U-boats were threatening to drive the Royal Navy from the seas and gain control of the Atlantic. Japan was moving toward open aggression in the Far East that challenged U.S. right in the Pacific. In November, 1940, President Roosevelt was elected to an unprecedented third term and on December 29th in one of his fireside chats he tried to reassure the nation by saying: "There is far less chance of the U.S. getting into war if we do all we can to support the nations defending themselves against the attack." But at 6 AM December 7th, 1041 Pearl Harbor was attacked. The President declared a state of was between the U.S. and Japan. Uncle Lowell was shipped to the Philippines, but dad had broken his arm and it hadn't healed correctly enough to hold a weapon properly. Instead, they sent him to Elgin Field to do his part by working in the shipyards. Uncle Lowell wasn't married, but dad was leaving behind a wife and three children. My grandparents began not only worrying about the war, but also how in the world we were going to make it without the two men.

While dad and Uncle Lowell were gone, some things remained the same. The KKK was alive and well and liked to remind people of that. Although there were hot beds of racial tensions in a lot of the cities we seemed to be untouched until one day we saw it firsthand. We had no idea of the evil they were capable of. One evening after supper grandpa was out on the porch smoking his pipe, watching us play hide-and-seek. We heard dogs in the distance getting closer with each bark. Grandma came out and said she was sure that it must be some poor black man being chased. She told us that dogs make different sounds when they are on a scent and for us to get in the house. About that time a young black man came running through the yard with terror on his face. Through the window we watched him begging grandpa to hide him. Grandpa told him the dogs would find him no matter where he hid him so the best thing to do was for him to walk through some water to hide his scent. Then, grandpa told him he would stall the men and dogs as long as he could. Then, grandpa told him he would stall the men and dogs as long as he could. We were scared to death.

A trio of young white teenagers, wielding knives, appeared and grandpa asked them if they were rabbit hunting. One replied: "Naw, we're after us a nigger. Did you see one run through here?" After grandpa denied seeing anyone, the one who seemed to be the leader, said: "I think you're lying old man and we're gonna show you just how sharp these knives are. Are we scaring you old man?" To their surprise out came grandma with a loaded shotgun and told them she would give them a head start and then find out how good a shot she was. She started shooting the sand around their feet. As they ran she fired over their heads while they were yelling that we would be sorry for this.

Sure enough, a week or so later, we awakened, to the smell of smoke. Thinking the house was on fire; the adults grabbed us and ran out. That was my very first time seeing a Klansman. Several of them stood around the perimeter of a huge cross burning in our yard. The rough cross was made from pine wrapped in rags and then drenched with gasoline. Although we couldn't see their faces, the hatred was palpable. What had we done to deserve this? After a time that seemed like an eternity, they faded into the night in their white robes and hoods. It was a very scary sight and left an indelible impression. My sisters and I didn't understand any of it. Grandpa tried to explain how some people didn't like other people just because of the color of their skin. Some of our happiest days had been spent with both black and white neighbors. Prejudice ignited a fire that burned our innocence.

During that horrible wartime, as kids, we did enjoy a few things but most were related to just the family getting by. Before winter could set in we spent many hours on neighbors' porches shelling pears and lima beans, canning tomatoes, okra and corn and in general enjoying each other's company. Grandma would promise us blackberry cobbler for supper if we each shelled a basket of black-eyed peas or butterbeans. After fishing, sometimes taking up to two days, we would grab out buckets and head to the fence line where the berries grew wild. The ladies would remind us to look for jimson weed while we were berry picking. We had picked it many times before because grandma said it helped her asthma. I guess all the ladies had asthma because all of them were delighted to get it. Years later I was told the weed was much like marijuana so I guess we had a pot-smoking granny. No wonder those ladies would cut loose with a jig now and then.

Other memorable times were when all the neighbors would get together to butcher and share the largest hog and cow. The meat was hung in a smoke house where slow burning hickory would cure it. They also made sausages which were stores in jars of lard that gave them flavor. The lard was made from rendering down the fat from the chosen hog. Jobs that I didn't particularly like included crawling under the house to get eggs laid by wandering chickens-spider webs everywhere-and going to the scary root cellar where the veggies were stored under the hay straw. I though snaked might have rested there for the winter. The best part of all this was getting to do the eating. The women collected all the organ meats and made hashlet for everyone to enjoy as it was considered to be a treat. This recipe was handed down through generations. Carrots, potatoes, onions and spices were added. That made dinner for all, served with biscuits and guava jam and lemonade made from our own fruit. They also made blood sausage, head cheese and pickled pigs' feet. Nothing was wasted. Southerners do love to eat.

The most fun days of all were when we piled into the back of a wooden wagon pulled by grandpa's mule and went to town to buy staples. Mom and grandma would sing and tell us stories about families crossing the country in covered wagons. It was easy to imagine we were a family going west.

Enjoying even the little things was soon to end, though I was not aware of it.

CHAPTER TWO
End of World War II

By April 1945 when Truman was President, the atomic bomb was nearly ready. On July 16th, Truman, Churchill and Stalin met in Potsdam for the final summit conference of the war. On that same day the atomic bomb was successfully tested in the desert near Alamogordo, New Mexico. On July 26 things really began heating up. A joint statement from the three leaders was issued as the "Potsdam Declaration", warning Japan of the uselessness of continued resistance. It ended with the warning that the only alternative was "prompt and utter destruction". Japan chose to ignore the declaration and thus sealed their fate.

A B-29 named "Enola Gay" headed for Japan's eighth largest city, Hiroshima. It was a military port and the home of Japan's war industries. The bomb was dropped at 8:15 AM, August 6, 1945. The formalities of surrender were held on the deck of the battleship "Missouri" anchored in Tokyo Bay, Sept. 2, 1945.

Our town was beginning to become more populated as med began returning from the war. We were looking forward to seeing dad and Uncle Lowell, but that was to be delayed because Uncle Lowell was sent to a hospital in the Carolinas. He needed recovery time. I heard the word "shell-shocked". I was eight years old now and "shell-shocked" was not part of my vocabulary.

Grandma and grandpa went on a Greyhound bus to visit their son but it was not a happy time. When they returned home they had little to say other than to warn us never to ask him any questions about the war when he got home. Apparently, it was a pretty big deal, because we would be punished if we did.

Our family grew sweet potatoes and cotton. We had to help pick the potatoes, but the thought of cotton picking was horrible. If you've never seen a cotton plant up close, I can testify that it is a nasty plant with four sharp points at the end of the flower. My sisters and I were spared from picking the cotton, but I felt so sorry for those who did have to pick it. Recently, when I visited in California who grows cotton crops, her son demonstrated al the latest equipment. His cotton picking machine had stereo and air conditioning as well as a hefty price tag. I have since wondered about what price was paid at the hands of cotton pickers of my time.

Dad finally came home to stay. He then got back into the swing of farm work. All we needed to get back to normal was Uncle Lowell.

Finally, Uncle Lowell was coming home and everyone was thrilled especially us kids. We felt close to him because he was unmarried and spoiled us rotten. We love him but we were particularly excited about hearing what he had to say about the war and to see if he brought us anything. He didn't disappoint us either. He gave me a grass skirt, he had been stationed in the Philippines. He picked me up to hug me and I asked him how many Japs he killed. I was about to find out what "shell-shocked" really meant to an eight-year-old. I was sent to m room with my mom and grandma hot on my trail. I was spanked and then had to stay in my room for thirty minutes for saying "Japs". I'm pretty sure I had heard it on the radio that my grandpa was glued to every night. The spanking wasn't so bad but it caught my attention.

Even though the beginning and end of the war as well as Uncle Lowell's misfortunes were life altering, the biggest change was yet to come. Our world, as we knew it, was about to turn upside down. Dad had gone to a tent meeting from which he came home with new beliefs and new plans. He had gotten "old time religion" and said he had spoken in tongues. He said it was electrifying, and he would never be the same. Truer words were never spoken but religion was only part of it. He and Uncle Lowell decided they could no longer be Alabama share-croppers but instead wanted to go to Florida to make their fortune. There the sun shined all the time. They had seen the light. They could pick oranges instead of cotton! Grandpa, who had always been a farmer, wasn't happy about the change of events and futilely tried to talk them out of it. They had seen a new future and would not be content down on the farm any longer. Without the help of his sons with the farm, grandpa had to come along.

Before long, there were more of us heading to Florida. My dad's only sister, Aunt Vee, lived in a small town a few miles away. She hadn't been in our lives very much except occasionally to visit grandpa and grandma. When she did visit, we were happy to play with our cousins. As time passed and we never saw their dad, Uncle Clyde, the boys let us know that he was a mean drunk. Unfortunately, I witnessed this be-havior on a trip home with them for a few days. We were sitting around the dinner table. Suddenly, Uncle Clyde burst into the room with a big knife held up in a threatening manner. We scattered out to the corn-field, hiding ourselves in the stalks. He followed us, stumbling around in the stalks and shouting for us to come out while still waving the knife around. He was a madman. We just knew we were going to die and probably would have had he found us. Eventually, he fell and didn't get up, sleeping it off. Dad picked up all of us the next day, six kids and Aunt Vee. She never went back. Before we left for Florida, Uncle Clyde showed up one day determined to take his wife and kids home. Dad and Uncle Lowell hadn't known the horror this man had put their sister through until fearfully, she let it all out. When they found out, they tied his feet together and hung him upside down over the well. They dunked his head in a few times, telling us they were playing a game with him. They said he liked it, but we didn't think he liked it.

One more incident meant the end of Uncle Clyde. After we had moved and been gone a year or so, he showed up to where Aunt Vee was now living. He began harassing and stalking her, threatening to kill her. He did fire a gun into her home one day, but thankfully, no one was hurt. He was eventually declared insane and spent many years in Chattahoochee, the Florida state mental institution. When he was released, he moved to Michigan and that's where he dies. Aunt Vee claimed his body and brought him home to bury in the family cemetery.

CHAPTER THREE
A New Start in Florida

Finally, the big day arrived and off we went looking like the "Beverly Hillbillies" or more correctly, the Alabama Hillbillies. Twelve people and a few boxes of our belongings packed into two old jalopies that the men had bought to be our chariots to our new life. After buying the cars there wasn't much money left for the trip which was a trip I will never forget. Of course, it was summer and if you have never experienced summer in the Deep South you don't know high humidity and sultry oppressive heat. Heat that makes you think your blood might boil. We were crammed into those old vehicles, sweating without heads hanging out the windows like dogs with their tongues blowing in the wind. Excitement soon turned into whining and crying – no air conditioning, no money for motels, having to use gas stations to wash up and eating peanut butter and jelly and spam and cheese sandwiches. The men took turns driving until one of the cars broke down. We were stuck for two days in a filthy gas station parking lot. The heat endured. You could have fried eggs on the hood of the car, if we had eggs. We found a little stand of trees across the road for a little shelter while the men took care of the car.

Finally, we were on the road again to our paradise. Trying to cheer things up, dad and Uncle Lowell spoke of the scent of magnolias, orange blossoms, southern jasmine and all the different fruits we could pluck off the trees at our leisure. To this day I can shut mu eyes and smell the orange blossoms when they bloom all through the state. It's mostly a memory, though, because when the groves froze so many times in the '80s many were plowed over and land was developed. Our trip that should have been traveled within 24 hours instead took us four days.

In 1947, dad, grandpa and Uncle Lowell all got jobs tending a newly planted grove. Because of their farming experience the owner was happy to have them. As part of their pay they were allowed to live in two houses situated at the edge of the grove. One was for grandpa, granny and Aunt Vee and her children. The other one was for dad, mom and us three girls and Uncle Lowell.

The men's job was to prune, plow and spray. They had a tractor and a truck to help them. I remember when they sprayed; they all came home with swollen eyes from the mist blowing back in their faces. When the temperatures were too low they had to put smudge pots amongst the trees to keep them from freezing. This meant staying out all night. I later learned it takes eight years before you get any fruit. Now don't complain about the cost of your orange juice, okay?

Grandma and Aunt Vee seemed to like it here. They didn't have nearly as much to do. All of us kids were like a litter of puppies having a ball exploring our new surroundings and discovering tangerines and other great things for the first time. Three of us, me and two of my cousins would be starting school soon.

My mother, however, was miserable and didn't like it there at all, "nothing, zip, zero," she said. Mom said our dad had turned into a "holy roller", he had decided he was going to be a preacher. He attended a local Pentecostal church and went to all the traveling tent meetings that came anywhere near us. They were everywhere at that time. Dad also attended an institute every Saturday in Orlando and sent away for many correspondence courses and expensive books. He was completely absorbed and totally neglectful of his family. Another sore spot was all the money he spent on this. Mother said many of these people prayed while they preyed on the poor and uneducated. Our mother was a very beautiful woman with a spirited personality. Grandma said she saw the beginning of the end of her son and his wife's relationship when he coerced us into accepting his beliefs. He insisted we wear long sleeves, hi-necked dresses, no lipstick for mom, no more Toni home perms, no nail polish. Mom couldn't even shave her legs anymore. Where in the Bible does it say that's a sin?

When dad was away working in Elgin Field coming home rarely, our mother would leave us in the care of our grandma and into town and spend the weekends with her brother, Uncle Jess and his wife, Aunt Margaret, for a few days of fun. I suppose they went out dancing and drinking as most young people do. I can understand why she liked to get away from the farm to enjoy this lively company and different atmosphere.

Eventually, during this time I Was later told, she met a man she never forgot. Dad had found a packet of letters from him, tied up with silk ribbon. There was a big confrontation. Mom said she was going back to Alabama to her family whom she missed. Dad said: "Fine, if you do, don't come back."

After a couple of weeks when she hadn't returned, he drove to where she was. He sweet-talked her into coming back home with him. She told grandma he promised to be more understanding of her feelings, and to ease up on all the restrictions. We girls were so happy to have her home, dad was dull, and mom was fun. She was a great seamstress. We have many treasured photos of us girls in matching dresses. They days were more fun, also the nights. In the evening she read us fairytales and tucked us in with a kiss goodnight. Big time changes were once again coming. These changes would impact us girls greatly for the rest of our lived. Dad found another letter from the same man that wrote the others. I never forgot it because he was the cause of our parent's final breakup. I'm sure it was made easier for our mother by dad's change into a religious fanatic. He stated that religion was his entire life. He stayed that way even though he wasn't always saintly, as you'll find out. He and I certainly clashed many times when I was older. Dad,

I was told many years later, was quite sure mom would respond to the letter and he was determined to intercept her answer. Years later, grandma and Aunt Vee said the contents were shocking, but would not tell me what it said. I wouldn't have understood anyway.

Years later when we were cleaning the house after dad's death, we found it. The letter expressed how unhappy she was with dad since he had become a religious fanatic. She said she hadn't planned on spending her life with "any preacher man". He had changed so much he wasn't the man she knew and loved once, and furthermore she was sick of living so far out in the orange grove that when she would climax, it was orange juice. Well, she had a wicked sense of humor, and when we read this we laughed in spite of ourselves. What we didn't understand, was why he kept it all those years. The letter had been the beginning of the end of their marriage.

CHAPTER FOUR
New Life

One morning at the breakfast table, dad told me to get dressed and help the younger ones I saw suitcases at the door. I asked who was going away. I was told: "your mother!" He said we were going to walk her to the cross road where a bus would pick her up. She was going to her home for a visit. To this day I haven't figured out why he took us along. It was a long walk in the sand, very hot and humid. I remember they quarreled and yelled at each other. When the bus pulled to a stop, I remember her saying to him: "Do not come after me I gave you a chance. You didn't try at all. I will never live in Florida again." When she hugged us goodbye dad said: "If not for me, won't you stay and help me raise these girls?" I think we realized something very wrong was happening. I was holding Carol's hand but she was trying to pull loose to go to "my mom" as she said. The baby, Gail, was on dad's shoulders and reaching for "her mom". I being older (nine I think) realized from a hurt deep inside this really was a serious matter, so when she sat down, looked out the window, I waved goodbye to "our mom". We wouldn't see that face again for fifteen years. There were no birthday cards, no Christmas cards, no gifts of homemade look alike dresses!

A few days later, the foreman of the groves that the men worked in stopped by to ask if they would relocate. He wanted them to start a new grove in the area of Clermont. He asked, but I don't think they really had a choice. It actually turned out to Ferndale, a small town near Clermont, about 30 miles from Orlando. They had saved enough money to buy a small house each where they lived the rest of their lives.

Aunt Vee had always wanted to be a nurse. She was so tired of packing fruit in boxes and mesh bags. So off she went to nursing school offered by one of Orlando's hospitals. She stayed in the apartments upstairs. She studied all day, and after some training, worked when she could. Granny watched all us kids, Aunt Vee came home on weekends. Once she finished and got her degree she worked for twenty years in one of Orlando's largest hospitals.

Dad said he hadn't told us yet, but he had been asked to take over as a pastor at a small country church in the same county. He said he would continue to work a few days a week because the congregation was quite small, but it did come with a parsonage. He planned on taking the position and moving there with us three girls. He said that I was old enough to help him with the two younger girls. As it turned out, we were overwhelmed with kindness. The members like their handsome, new preacher. The ladies were always bringing casseroles, cookies, etc. to the house. The men kept all the property mowed, windows washed, etc.

The carefree days were gone. I was in 6th grade, I believe. Even with dad and the members helping out, that was the end of my childhood even after he remarried, I had big responsibilities. Because of this, I still have the terrible trait of a take charge attitude/ Do it my way and everything will be just fine. I am strong willed, but if you treat me right, you'll be treated likewise. I am known by all my friends to have a gentle nature, and if you need my help I'll be there for you.

I did notice the younger, prettier women would use any excuse to come over. A preacher is not blind to this. Dad was a bit of a flirt. After a woman walking out on you, I'm sure this was flattering. After about a year he zeroed in on one he chose to marry. She must have had hidden talent.

CHAPTER FIVE
Dad's New Wife

A favorite date for dad and his soon-to-be-wife was to go hear well-known gospel quartets sing. Dad owned an old truck. He and Dottie would sit up front, of course No matter the weather, unless it was stormy, we were under quilts in the back. I don't remember ever being asked about homework and quite often we didn't get home until 11:00pm. I really don't know why we had to go with them anyway.

The courtship didn't last long. One Sunday after church another minister married them. Our family now numbered five. My sisters and I were happy to have a real family like other kids. Now we had a mom again, finally. Dad had a long talk with us before they married about what he expected from us. So we were trying very hard to be on our best behavior. We didn't have to try hard because we were basically good kids. Those hell fires and brimstone sermons on Sunday had apparently done the job. How bad could we possibly be? We had been loved. We weren't prepared for what followed. Dottie appeared to be crazy about dad, but it became crystal clear she didn't love us. She didn't even like us. She especially hated me, and it never stopped. However, when she realized she was dying she begged me to forgive her. I'm not one to believe in being evil all your life, and at the last minute say: "oops! By the way, I'm sorry about that." She epitomized the evil step-mother of lore and then some more. We were told by her never to call her "mom". She said: "I'm not your mom and you must be real brats or your mother wouldn't have left you. You can call me Dot." Our world would never be remotely anywhere close to the way it was.

Dot didn't think she could have children, but she did eventually become pregnant three times. The first one she miscarried, the second only lived a few days as did the third one. After each birth she was even meaner toward us. I believe the reason she kept getting meaner was because she lost her babies and there we were, some other woman's children whom she didn't want when she couldn't have her own. I was even more confused as to why dad allowed her to treat us the way she did. Wouldn't you think she would be happy to have three little girls?

She was very heavy and had diabetes for which she took medicine, but she ate all the wrong things like cake, pie, ice cream, etc. I never saw her try to lose weight. I never understood this attitude. She would die at forty-one, blind and missing part of a leg.

Dot worked in a plant, sectioning fruit for canning. She worked a split shift so she wore two different dresses each day. I had to wash, starch and hang them on the line to dry, then sprinkle with water and iron them. We didn't have steam irons back then. I also had to make sure dad had five white dress shirts ready all the time, plus our clothes for school. I mentioned this because she made us girls wear the same dress two days in a row. We tried to get her to let us rotate since we weren't allowed to wear five different dresses. I didn't put up a fuss the first year. But the next year, I would dress the two younger ones, Carol and Gail, in different outfits and try to sneak them out the door. If Dot caught me, she would raise cane and actually try to get them back in the house to change, but I would tell them to run, and I would hold her back. My middle sis said later she remembers me taking many licks for her and Gail. For myself, I thought, so what, clothes and shoes don't matter. It's the person. Besides that I was fifteen and I only had a few more years and I'd be out of there. I was intelligent and had a good personality. I was elected to the student council. I sang in the glee club and played on the basketball team as a forward. The day I was chosen for the basketball team I was so happy, but couldn't figure out how I would get home after the games which were played after school let out. One of the girls told me her mother would drop me off because they drove by the turn-off near my house. I was so excited and proud of myself because I had scored once in that afternoon game. I couldn't wait to show dad my uniform. I was happy that at last I would have something fun to do and be a part of my school's activities. When he saw it was shorts he said: "you know you can't wear those so take the uniform back". We even had to do P.E. in our dresses. Somehow I thought this would be different.

I had to get up in the mornings before everyone else to make breakfast which would be home-made biscuits that granny taught me to make. We would butter them and pour sorghum molasses over the warm biscuits. Once in a while we were lucky if we had bacon or sausage. Later on we had chickens and it was wonderful to have plenty of fresh eggs. Of course there was always fruit right outside the door.

While the rest of the family ate, I made up the two beds. Then, it was brush teeth, get dressed and walk half a mile to the bus stop. When we got home: cook dinner, wash dishes and do my homework and help the girls with theirs. If it was a church night we had to go even if exams were the next day. I fell asleep many time at the kitchen table studying. I was determined to better myself. I dreamed of when I could get started to make my life my own. Our weekends weren't much better; church in the morning, home for lunch, relax a bit, and then back to evening services at seven. It was ten o' clock before we got home most of the time. I was getting along on just 6 hours of sleep most nights. During the week we had Bible study one night, youth activities one night and services twice on Sunday. I never went to a church after I grew up that had evening services. I also now prefer a non-denominational church.

I always had a talent for art, so that was my salvation. I could lose myself in that and get praise for the results. I did seasonal drawings with colored chalk on our homeroom blackboard. The best one was Rudolph pulling Santa in a sleigh. I once had a write up in the church pamphlet of a picture I did of Jesus in the Garden of Gethsemane. The art definitely helped me cope. I spent any free time I had drawing or painting. I had a varied, beautiful collection that I Was very proud of. A school counselor once told me if I continued the way I was going, maybe I could get into art school on a scholarship. That was certainly exciting to think about. I should never have mentioned this at home because one Saturday afternoon, I saw Dot throwing paper one-by-one into the burn barrel. Finally it got my interest up and I ventured outside to see. She was throwing my artwork in and when she saw me she dumped what was left into the blaze. I don't care how strong I thought I was that just about did me in. I didn't paint again for a long time.

Life rocked along as usual. I can't remember dad's reaction to the art fire. Nothing changed so it must not have been profound. I can tell you I was getting more than fed-up with Dot, and even more so at Dad for not standing up and helping our family such as it was. What could I have ever done to make her treat me this way? I still mourn the loss of my early work.

I was never able to paint that well again. I never lost my love for art, though. I later studied sculpting for five years, becoming an award-winning artist.

The next incident with Dot was forever burned into my soul, and dad took part. I wasn't going to take abuse from her ever again. I had protected the smaller ones as best I could so she dared not even go near them in a threatening manner. I realized it was obvious dad wasn't going to do anything. One day after a big blow-up he said: "I wash my hands of you both. I don't want to hear anymore from you when I get home." Then he did something for which we three girls never forgave him.

We got home from church one Sunday and some chickens were lying dead in the yard. A hole was dug under the wire at the chicken coops. We had never had a pet before and a few months earlier we were visited by a small pup that stayed. I can tell you we three girls loved that dog with all our hearts. He was so cute and playful. We named him, Buster. Dot had convinced dad the dog had to be shot because we relied on the eggs and meat. She said Buster would do it again. We were young, but we even realized there were other solutions, which we pointed out later: let us find a new home for one. But no, Dot had her way. When we realized he was going to get his gun and when he headed out into the yard, we ran out and hugged the dog to protect hum, but we were ordered back into the house. I'm not sure if Dot had said "Shoot them all" he wouldn't have. He had lost his mind as far as I was concerned. We three ran into our bedroom and heard a shot ring out. We looked out the window and we saw him shoot a second shot that sent the pup tumbling and roll over dead. I think a bit of us died that day. After a while we went out, put the pup in a boxy and buried him along with our hearts in a grave piled with stones and marble. We put flowers on there every day after school. I have been dreading to write about this because when someone damages your soul, it never heals. I weep today just as painfully as I did the day it happened. I hated them both for what they did, because they could have spared us the pain we still carry by simply giving him to someone who would have loved him for the sweet baby he was/ Besides, as we tried to point out, we had foxes, raccoons, etc. It would have hurt enough to give him away but the pain wouldn't be as raw. It was flat out war after that. We were living with two crazy people. Years later when we were grown women with children of our own, the dog incident came up. We all hugged and cried and promised to never mention it again. Nobody was ever going to hurt me again.

If Dot slapped me, she got one right back. If she was yelling at me or calling me names and happened to be near a bed or chair, she was shoved on to it. I talked back to her, even called her an ugly big fat cow. She said: "I'm going to tell your dad" and I replied: "Go ahead, who cares." I had become a strong person and stayed that way the rest of my life, not mean, just strong.

Honestly, dad seemed almost oblivious to the drama in the house. If he wasn't at work, his head was in a book preparing for the next service. If I ever tried to talk to him about Dot and my problems, it didn't do any good. He quite often would say: "I just don't know why the two of you can't get along." That was always so confusing to me. How could you be a preacher and not be a good family man? He was standing in the pulpit every Sunday telling others how to live better lives. However, you only have to listen to the news or read a paper to know there are a lot of high profile married men of God that are being exposed for indulging in many of the behaviors they themselves preach against. [Greed, fraud, soliciting prostitutes (male and female)] This, of course caused me to questions my dad as a spiritual leader; to allow what was going on in his own house, and then on Sunday preach the love of God and your fellow man. All I saw was a weak man who shot his children's pet because his wife told him to. All three of us girls were turned off religion for many years. Later in life we would visit him on his birthday. We all had colored our hair, shaved our legs, wore shorts and one was smoking and we all had a Jack Daniels in our hand. With his crooked finger pointing in disbelieve he admonished: "Don't know how I raised you like I did and you live like you do."

We didn't stay long.

Dot had a sister named Judy who was two years older than I. She would spend weekends with us once in a while. By the way, the rest of Dot's family was very nice to us. How her evil sperm got passed the guards, I can't imagine. I know she never did one worthwhile deed to make the world a better place.

I soon learned about the birds and the bees from Judy. Her boyfriend would drive over to take her out and I got to tag along. We usually went to the drive-in movies, which I wasn't supposed to do. But I wasn't going by dad's and Dot's rules any longer. I didn't believe in the teachings of that religion anyway. After the movie and burger we headed home. About halfway home, they pulled off the road and went back into an orange grove. He parked the car and they got out taking a blanket from the trunk and disappeared into the grove. That night I talked to Judy about this when we went to bed, asking her all kinds of questions which she seemed to have the answers. I didn't even really know what menstruation was all about. When I asked Dot about it she said: "It's something women do once a month for a few days." She said: "If you don't you're pregnant." She also said that you need to tear up some old rags and stick them in your panties. She never bought me any sanitary pads so I did without lunch to buy them out of the machine in the girl's restroom. I could not believe Judy was doing "the wild thing". I asked if she wasn't afraid of getting pregnant. "No," she said, because he used rubbers," as they were called then. I could not fathom how this was done until she explained it. Gross! So use protection, she said. I didn't have any plans of a man crawling on top of sideways or however it was done until I had a marriage license.

One time when her boyfriend came over, he brought a friend for me. His name was George. The only reason I was allowed to go out was because Dot wanted us girls married ASAP. She still couldn't help herself. When George walked me up to the door, I saw her through the blinds, run the clock ahead. At first I thought she was checking to see if I was late. When I came into the house she would show dad and tell him: "We let her go out and she won't even abide by the curfew." This meant I couldn't go the next week-end. I never argued with this. What was the use? But she knew that I knew because I would tell her the next day what a creep she was. When my middle sis started dating, she said she would come home when she damned well felt like it because she was going to be restricted anyway.

My first real date with George, no Judy or Hugh, I felt quite grown up. I was sixteen, he was twenty-two. Would you let your daughter go out with a man six years older than her? The evening was going fine, that is, until the orange grove. If he thought I was like Judy he was in for a surprise and I was totally shocked that he assumed as much. After that he and some buddies would stop by occasionally on Saturday or Sunday afternoon driving motorcycles. Some of them had girls, but I certainly wasn't allowed to do that. George did apologize and we went out a couple more times. I had a mad crush on a young man (boy) that lived nearby and he was my age. This was Puppy live, the way it should be, not a twenty-two year old taking you into an orange grove.

The final blow-up happened one evening at the dinner table. We were all quiet, eating our meal, when out of the blue, Dot slapped me across the face so hard my chair fell over and my head hit something and started bleeding heavily. I hadn't said or done a thing. Even dad, for a change, said: "What the hell did you do that for?" The biscuits should have been cornbread or she didn't like what I cooked, who knows. As I got up, she said: "Let me see that cut." I said for her to keep her nasty hands off. "Don't you dare touch me." This was especially hurtful because I had talked to the two younger ones about having everything perfect that evening so there would be peace in the house. They agreed and had even picked wildflowers for the table. Maybe, that was it; I was trying to be miss perfect and was growing into a pretty girl that, I was told, looked like my mother. When this happened, I knew I was leaving the next day. I hadn't thought it through yet. I couldn't take it anymore that I knew for sure.

I ran out of the house and hid in the grove up in a grapefruit tree, my second home. I had even cleaned up around it, raking underneath. I had also clipped the branches so it was easier to climb. I would dream of my prince charming galloping through the orange grove and sweeping me up and away. I usually stayed there until their bedroom light went out when sis would use a flashlight to let me know it was clear. I would climb in the window. When I think of all this, it's amazing we were sane. While sitting in the tree like a dang monkey I would pray. A calmness came over me and a voice said: "You're going to have the life you want one day so stay strong." The grove was a dark and eerie place with strange noises and some scary things, like spiders, large spiders, large spiders and snakes that didn't make noise, but you saw in the day time so you knew they were there. The trees also had thorns, but I had cleaned this one up somewhat. I also knew the gators crawled through the groves to the many lakes that were in the area, so I felt safer up in the tree than on the ground. I heard a noise then saw a figure with a gun. I relaxed because I knew that men hunted animals at night for extra food. Then, I heard dad's voice calling my name. I thought how nice it would be for him to hold me and say how sorry he was and from then on our life would be better. He wasn't the hugging type. No I love you. No kisses, no hugs. It wouldn't have made a difference anyway. He had never came out looking for me before! I'd had it and I wasn't going to stay another day. As I was thinking of climbing down to tell him this, a voice, so crystal clear, said three words to me: "DO NOT MOVE". I didn't and it's haunted me all my life.

Aunt Vee had given me a cedar chest (they were called "hope chests") on my sixteenth birthday. Southern girls would make quilts, pillowcases and table cloths which we embroidered with flowers on vines to put away for marriage.

This last run in with Dot sent me out of the house running home to grandpa and grandma, never to go back. Until then they hadn't known how bad it was at our house. Although they knew Dot and I didn't get along, I never told them details. They never liked her and couldn't understand why their son married her. They were too old to burden with such non-sense. And dad was so bedazzled that I don't think a talk from them would have changed anything anyway. The next morning was a Saturday. I called George asking if he would drive me to my grandma's house. He said he would, so I put my meager belongings in the chest. When dad saw I was determines to leave, he wrote a note for me to deliver to his mother saying "Dot and Tina are at it again. I will be over after church tomorrow to get her." Grandma lived about twenty miles away. After I told granny what was going on in our house, she dressed her son up one side and down the other, telling him I would most certainly not be going back to that. I never did!

I was worried about the younger ones. But the assured me she did not mistreat them. George and I would pick them up on Friday after school, returning them on Sunday. I know they would have broken down and told me if Dot was mistreating them.

I would have to change schools because granny was in a different district. We were on summer break at this time. Before school started grandma was diagnosed with stomach cancer. Terminal, the doctor was saying a year at the most.

So the powers that ruled over me said I was to stay home and take care of her. I couldn't argue with that because they all had to work, plus I loved her deeply. So, I was fine with that. I could pick up my schooling later. My plans were still there, just on hold.

It was a pleasure to care for grandpa and grandma so I could give back a bit of what they had given me. She lasted almost a year, dying with me sitting on the side of her bed fanning her. Gramps was sitting nearby. I said "granddaddy I think she's gone." He came over, kissed her on the forehead, closed her eyes and laid a coin on each eyelid. This was my first time seeing someone die. If my heart wasn't broken before this, it was now, because I loved her above all others and knew she loved me. Later on I would find a baby gown with a note saying: "Use this to take your first born home from the hospital." I did, and then framed it.

Grandma had told everyone she wanted me to have her little house because I was taking care of her and had agreed to take care of grandpa. The house wasn't much, but the land around it was beautiful. They had lemons, limes, pomegranates, guava and kumquats that she candies.

It didn't take long after grandma died for dad and Dot to give up their "free" home and move in. God forbid I should get the house and land. They said for me to get out of "their" house. They were going to care for grandpa. Aunt Vee was working to support herself and her daughter. Uncle Lowell and Aunt Myrtice were expecting a baby so neither had much input into caring for grandpa.

They were pushing me to marrying George. I had to legal right to the house because it wasn't yet on paper and I did not intend to be around Dot anymore, period. All I asked for was one of her hand-made quilts when she died. I didn't get it.

CHAPTER SIX
New Husband

I felt trapped. So, one day, George and I went to the courthouse and a judge married us. I cried not because of happiness. I was just a piece of furniture to George. The sex, I wouldn't call it "making love", was "wham, bam, thank you ma'am". I wondered what all the fuss was about. I'm sure a lot of the problem was mine. Too young for one and the closeness was uncomfortable. I got pregnant the first time I think, because I had a baby nine months later. I didn't have an easy nine months. I was anemic, weighing only 95 pounds. When I was sent to the hospital a second time, the doctors said I should abort the fetus because I wasn't healthy enough to carry full term. I was young and there would be other babies, "Think about it and we'll talk tomorrow." I was lying there so confused, thinking about all this. I had been told that when you're about half-term the baby starts to move. I was about that far along and hadn't felt any movement yet. I didn't know what to do. I said, out loud, as I held my stomach: "Hey little one, what a predicament we're in. You need to help me here." I fell asleep that way and was awoken with a kick. He's still kicking at 55. It turned out; he would be my only child. I am very grateful to have him. I did not want to get pregnant again so I made sure I didn't. I was on my way out as soon as I could come up with a plan. I started putting money away, which was easy because George never knew how much he had spent when he went out with the boys. He didn't care about family life. He was still living like a single guy. He was spending his money on guns and hunting dogs, a cabin cruiser for fishing and a party boat. He had a good job cleaning the inside of big steel tanks that held juice for bottling. The guys all hung out at the bars after work, going home when they felt like it. You'd hear them say: "Keep your woman's belly full of babies and she'll be so busy. She'll leave you alone." Not this girl/woman. I knew the life I had dreamed of was waiting for me out there somewhere. I guess I had lessons yet to learn before I could have it. I never lost faith.

George's brothers told him, he'd better start acting like a married man or I was surely going to leave. Little did they know I was leaving no matter what. I was just an object of George's pleasure, just like his toys. I hadn't fallen in love, so it was easy to leave. So, after two years of this life, I picked up my child and caught a bus to Orlando, about forty miles away to start the new phase of my life. I had just turned twenty.

CHAPTER SEVEN
On My Own

I had picked up a newspaper a month earlier to look for a housemate to share expenses. I found one who was also had a two year old boy. I went to meet her and we got along okay. So, Rusty and I had a new home in a very nice neighborhood on a shady street. We had a newspaper boy, milk delivery, garbage pick-up, street lamps and policemen. I was making progress in the way I wanted to live and bring up my son. It was wonderful; we were on our way to a better life. It was a bit overwhelming but I had what I wanted. My life was now my own.

Our landlord was a nice old gentleman who lived over the garage and soon became "Pappy" to the two little boys, and a friend to me. I then set about finding a job for me and daycare for Russ. I found work packing mail-order for Florida Fashion. I stayed there till I turned twenty-one.

When my middle sister left home and came to live with me, I got my own place and she took care of Rusty.

One night George broke into the house in a drunken rage, demanding I go home with him. Not to you fellows; coming over with chocolate and flowers works better. By the time he stormed out, I had bruises, a swollen eye and marks on my neck. I called the police, but since we weren't divorced, they called it a lovers' quarrel. It's different now, thankfully. They did say to go the next day to the police station and after pictures were taken, I could then swear out a warrant for his arrest.

I was scared to do so but damn it, I wasn't going to let him get away with it. It wasn't just me; it was doing that in front of our son. I hear later, he was picked up at his job. I don't know what happened; some jail time I hope. Later on, when he was called to meet me at the attorney's office to sign some papers, he tore them up and threw them on the desk, saying he didn't want the divorce and stomped out. I think, by then, he did want the divorce. He just didn't want to pay for it, but I did. I never received any child support which I didn't push because I was sure I could use this to my advantage sooner or later. I was sooner than I expected.

I let Russ go home with George for a weekend visit. I was told by his family that they would look out for him. Come Sunday evening, he hadn't returned my three year old son. I could not take a day off. I wouldn't have a free say until Wednesday. I didn't own a car so I had to take a bus to the town where he lived and a taxi to his residence. Needless to say, I was mad.

When I arrived a young girl was sitting on the floor, playing with Rusty. He jumped up and ran to me. She asked: "Who are you?" "I'm his mother and I have to come get him." She told me I couldn't do that. She was in charge of him. I Replies that her services were no longer needed and if she didn't live there, she needed to go home, and I left with my son. How aggravating to spend my day off this way, spending extra money when I shouldn't have to.

Rusty and I usually had a fun day planned that included riding our bikes to the park to feed the ducks, and going to a nice restaurant later (teaching dinner manners) and to a movie and then caught a bus home. We had a dish of ice-cream, prayers and beddy-bye, as he called it. How wonderful to be in charge of my life. I loved it, knowing a great future was waiting for me.

I was able to get George's visitation rights stopped. I found out on the last visit, he and his buddies had taken Rusty out on his boat which he wasn't supposed to do because of his drinking. I get sick when I think about what could have happened. He came over a few times to see him but that soon stopped. I think some men care more about aggravating the ex-wife than they care about the children.

I had met a few waitresses who worked at the two top hotels in Orlando. The San Juan was in the downtown district, The Cherry Plaza was on Lake Eola. They made very big tips. They had to because at the time there were no minimum wage laws. They received a dollar a meal. With all the arrogance of youth, I walked into the San Juan, choosing that one because it was near the bus stop. Thank goodness they needed a new girl. They must have thought I had experience and I would discretely follow another waitress around for a week. I was so relieved they didn't say: "You can start tomorrow night." I was quite nervous being in such an elegant atmosphere. I thought, how difficult can it be. I did feel like this is where I belonged at the moment. It was a beautiful place to work, such a long way from the limb of a grapefruit tree. I enjoyed the job and did make enough money to live on. I was never able to afford a car but the bus stop was nearby. Our uniforms were kept washed, ironed and hung back up in our closets by the hotel maids. Our uniforms were black with white collar, cuffs and apron. We were expected to keep our hair and nails neat at all times, so we went upstairs to the salon quite often. The job was very easy. We each had six tables with a busboy assigned to numbered sections. A short meeting was held by the hostess before we opened to discuss any special events for the evening, then we were given our section number. When the order was taken it was given to a kitchen steward who then relayed it to the head chef. We weren't allowed to speak to the chefs at all. When your order was nearly ready, the bus boy would come tell you to complete what you're doing because he would bring your order out for your table in five minutes. The busboys always cleaned and reset the table. I don't know what the busboys were paid, but we were expected to tip them heavily, also throw in a five dollar bill at the end of the week for the hostess. If you were smart, you handed the kitchen steward a brown bag once in a while, ahead of the game, if you knew what his favorite was. The chefs were happy with a good quality wine. It really was a first class place. We were often given flowers, candy, perfume etc. from the customers. I remember once getting a large bottle of Shalamar and my boyfriend at the time poured it down the toilet. That was the end of him. The gist was not from a man trying to get my attention; it was a table of local businessmen. How stupid and immature. Now you know how a proper kitchen is run, on booze, good wine, good food and tips.

It didn't take me long to apply for the next opening upstairs in the piano lounge. I grabbed the chance to work if a girl had a late date after nine, because after nine, Rusty would be asleep and the babysitter liked to make extra money. Why go through the whole formal dining routine when you could make more money just serving cocktails? You didn't have to share your tips either because the customers at the bar tipped the bartenders. You wouldn't believe how sharp they dressed. I was so happy to be in such a nice place. I was holding my own; no one guessed I had just walked out of the orange groves a year ago.

A wild coincidence was Dot's older glamorous sister, Rene, worked in the hotel beauty shop. I stopped in to see her and got my hair done. She said she had just gotten back from Montego Bay where she went with a boyfriend. Rene was beautiful in a cool sophisticated sort of way. She gave me the complete beauty treatment at no charge. Later on, we shared a house and Russ stayed home. She and I together hired a housekeeper.

There was a businessman's convention in town and the shop was full of gorgeous girls getting themselves ready for the evening. The conversation was lively and raunchy. They had ordered Bloody Marys brought up to the shop. They asked if I Wanted one, but I refrained, having never drunk before. I always wondered why a drink was given that name. On my first date I was trying to appear cool and worldly. Even though I knew drink names, I didn't know how strong they were. When my date ordered, I said: "The same please." He ordered a Man-hattan- WHOA! I quickly learned about hi-balls.

When the girls in the beauty salon heard I worked downstairs, they said I was too young and pretty to sling hash, as they put it. They were sure they boss would hire me. Did I Want them to call New York and ask? I said "No thanks" to the offer, knowing by then they were call girls, working the Eastern Seaboard islands. I wondered about Rene! I didn't think she could own a house on Lake Butler and drive a new Cad every year on a hairdresser's salary and tips.

Some of the girls traveled with a maid/babysitter. They said they owned apartments in New York and shared a condo in the Bahamas. They laughed at me when I said, "NO!" I wouldn't have done it anyway, but I thought what would your grown children say later? I got the last laugh when I saw them coming into the dining room with some of the "fugliest" big, fat, red-nosed men I ever saw. There were a few nice-looking ones, but many more of them had to pay to have a beauty on their arm. If you judge on a scale of 1-10; then 1-7 doesn't have to pay-so what's left? Women out there watch your men closely. It is difficult for them to resist a beautiful woman who had nothing else in the world on her mind except pleasing him for a few hours, and for big bucks, I'm told. I suppose they put it on their expense accounts.

That was not the way I planned for my life to be. Life was going well and I Was having fun for the first time ever.

Then, I got a case of the stupids. Into my life walked the most charming and irresistible man. After work, once in a awhile, us girls would go next door to a popular hangout for young people our age. They had a great little band. I love the saxophone so I had a crush on the sax player. On his break he would sit with me, but we hadn't gone out because of our working hours.

Then in walks Hal. The ultimate playboy, as it turned out, racking up notches on his belt. I saw him there several times, but ignored his glances. I knew he would make a move sooner or later. I think he knew I had him figured out, so he came on like a true gentleman. He hung onto your every word making you think you're the only girl in the room. So different from a lot of the guys who were always looking over your shoulder when they danced to see if something better had walked in. And, he was certainly different than George.

Hal was a Sgt. At the Orlando Air Force Base, so we went to the N.C.O. Club quite often. He was very nice to Rusty, bringing him games, watching him ride his bike, teaching him to fly a kite and taking him out for burgers, fries and milkshakes. I hadn't been down this road before, so it was kind of fun.

The hormones are quite a bit different in a woman of 22 and a girl of 16 or 17. He taught me love making instead of sex-making. IT wasn't easy but he was patient with me, saying: "If I can't please you then I'm not happy." Nice Guy, huh? Wrong. I was married and divorce in one year. And what a year it was. New orders, so hand on here we go to Keesler Air Force Base in Biloxi, Mississippi. We got married before we left. Dad did the honors, convenient.

My middle sister, Carol, had babysat for me when she lived with us and was upset about me leaving. She felt Russ was part hers. Dad was also upset about his "little man" leaving. Rusty loved his pawpaw and was sad also. I never got over the way he had treated us. But I wasn't going to keep Russ from knowing him. He would know a different man than I did. Actually, Carol had opened a daycare center that was doing quite well, so they talked me into leaving Russ for a few weeks until I found an apartment and settled in. It was going to be a long time before they would see him again, they said. Plus, he had two cousins he already knew in the play group. He loved his Aunt Carol and said he wanted to stay for a while, but I better hurry back.

We were going by rail so I was excited about that, not having ever been on a train or trip before. We were going to get off in Montgomery, Alabama to visit with his mother and stepfather for a couple days. When the cab pulled up in front of a stately old southern home, I was surprised. I don't know what I expected. We were warmly welcomed and had dinner in the formal dining room served on beautiful china dishes by a cook who came in and out very quietly with wonderful food from she-crab soup to apple pie with aged cheddar.

After dinner the very first night, Hal announced he was going to his favorite hangout to meet some friends he had called. I asked if I could come along. He said: "No, get acquainted with mom." I thought it bad manners to leave his mom the first night, especially since I didn't know her. Of course, this made me mad and suspicious, because I knew he had a girlfriend there. I heard his mother tell him she was very surprised and upset when she heard he had gotten married. His mom, her husband and I sat on the veranda. It was very pretty, decorated with white wicker furniture and hanging baskets of begonias. We had a good visit and they were nice people. When they excused themselves to go inside, I asked if she knew the name of her son's favorite haunt. When she told me, I called a cab and went there. Nobody told me what I could and couldn't do. Big mistake, I just wanted to see if he was with her before we left. If he was-he only had to tell me he wanted to talk with her. I slipped in with a group and went to the farthest barstool. When my eyes adjusted, I saw Hal sitting way in the back being lovey-dovey.

His mother had told me that he receives a check from his father's trust every so often and if I personally ever needed money let her know. I had often wondered how he drove a new Oldsmobile, wore "after six" evening wear, expensive watch etc. on a staff Sgt.'s pay. Now I knew I had married a spoiled first class playboy.

When he got home that night, I was asleep, but not for long. He had seen me in the bar and was in a rage. I was shocked and scared when he started beating up on me. I was trying to calm him down and keep quiet out of embarrassment, being in his mother's home. And, but they way, where were they when I finally got out of the room crying loudly? The next morning no one said a word about what happened. After breakfast I went by cab to the bus station. About 100 miles down the road I got to thinking, I had given up my job and apartment. I didn't have enough money to get started again, so I took a cab back. I had come up with a plan.

When we started looking for an apartment, Hal only wanted to look at one bedroom units. I reminded him we needed two bedrooms. I guess he thought he was irresistible and I was stupid enough to give up my child and get beat up, too. In regards to the apartment, he said:

"I've been meaning to talk to you about that. I really don't like children, as a matter of fact; I had a vasectomy so I wouldn't have any. You should leave your child where he is. You and I can make life one big party." I said: "Are you serious!" and he said: "Dead Serious", and plopped down two month's rent. What a jerk! And what a dummy I was for not seeing through him. I figured this one would suit him just fine. I was there for two nights when I put my plan to work. Because of the move he had a lot of cash on him, so I helped myself and then some extra for the Alabama incident. A young couple lived upstairs and I asked them if they could tell me the names of three or four of the best hotels across from the ocean. They did, so I called and set up interviews for the next afternoon. I found a place to stay for the night.

When I went out the next morning in search of food, I saw a help-wanted sign in a small bar window. From the outside it looked nice enough, so, I went in. Not knowing if I would nail down any of the interviews I had scheduled for the afternoon, I was pointed to a door, heard "come in" and was asked questions by a slimy creature. "Are you qualified?" "Yes, I Am" "Are you a 'B' girl?" "I guess not, since I don't know what a 'B' girl does." "She flirts around, keeping the guys drinking and buying watered-down drinks." "I wouldn't do that" I told him. "Well, what are you waiting for? You wanting a job upstairs where the real money is?" "What's up there?" I asked. "Beds," he said. That was my exit word. Honest to God, I thought he was going to say where the more elite meet to drink quietly. I was not familiar with the military town. I later heard there were 40,000 service men there.

That afternoon I called a cab, went by the apartment and packed my things. I made a deal to hire the driver for the afternoon. I had the interviews lined up an hour apart, so off we went and I was entering a new phase of my life. I had enough money to last me until I found work, so I wasn't too worried. I guess it's a good thing that we can't know what's ahead of us. IT seemed to me that no matter what you do, a path is laid out or I wasn't making good decisions, just working my tail off to stay out of the bad ones I was making. Life was about to get very scary, *life threatening scary.*

All four of the hotels were beautiful and I chose to work at the one that gave me a room with a view of the gulf and dinner each evening. I would be working in a cozy downstairs cabaret called The Julep Room, famous for what else; cold mint juleps and hot jazz. I was elated, now I could start straightening out the mess I had made and get myself home to Orlando and Russ. A very nice couple ran the place. They took me under their wings and we worked well together. Our days were free to do as we pleased and hanging out at the pool was a favorite. A lot of interesting people lived there. A lot of high ranking military officers and at the time some Royal Canadian Air Force guys were there for some kind of special training. They loved to Bar-B-Que out back on weekends saying they were going to teach the Canadians how to make southern BBQ when they got home. Throw in some call girls, and then dancers, singers, male and female strippers and you know our after hour parties were legendary. For a girl raised like me, I thought I was in adult Disney Land. Just take the elevator home, sleep it off and start over the next day. By the way, Hal hadn't found me yet. I loved that he hadn't and smiled when I thought of how confused he must be that a woman would actually leave him.

I had not been living there long, when I started getting raunchy, filthy, phone calls from men telling me what they expected me to do to them and what they were going to do to me. After a few days of this, I'm wondering what to do when one evening I was eating dinner in the corner of the Julep Room, the decision was made for me.

Four or Five steps led down to The Julep Room from a circular drive. I saw a long black limousine pull up, and then heard banging on the door. The bartender went to tell them that we weren't open yet. They asked if a girl named "Tina" worked there. When the answer was "yes", the shoved past the bartender. They then saw me, walked over looking like they came right of central casting for The Sopranos. They asked: "Are you Tina?" I asked: "Who wants to know?" "The Dixie

Mafia Honey" as he played with a piece of rope laced through a chain. The other one said: "Stupid little bitches like you, who come into town on their own and don't like to follow the rules, get tossed into Lake Pontchartrain, with a concrete block tied around their neck making pretty fish food." The other one grinned and continued twisting the rope and chain. I was very scared, hoping they didn't decide to yank me out of my chair right then. As they turned to leave, they said to the bartender: "You three better get smart, you're playing with the wise guys." They were enjoying themselves, acting out their role. The bartender asked: "What the hell was that all about." I replied: "I don't know but they scared the crap out of me." So we called the police and they put two detective on the job. They were around, in and out, for a couple of weeks before they solved the mess I had gotten myself into without knowing what I had done. – Have you solved it yet? –

The cabbie thought I was going into hotels turning tricks when I was going in for my interviews. He was sending work my way and I wasn't kicking back. I had seen him at the bar a few time and said "Hello". I assume that's when money was supposed to pass.

Then one day, I looked up and what do I see? My New Orleans buddies coming over to help me eat dinner. They said "Hi, sweetie. We came to offer you a job at the Playboy Club in New Orleans where you will be making a lot more money, maybe find a 'sugar daddy', cute as you are." I ignored them and they asked: "Cat got your tongue?" I said: "You scared me half to death, you can kiss my ass." As they turned to leave, they said: "Oh baby, we would love to!" "Go back to your rat hole and leave me alone." I never saw them again. No more phone calls.

A few days later, some of the strippers came and asked me if I wanted to come and watch them practice their routine for the night's show. They said: "Maybe you'd prefer to be a stripper rather than a cocktail waitress. Make more in three hours than the seven you work." I said: "I wasn't about to strut half-naked up and down a bar and let guys stuff money in my panties.

They said they didn't work in that kind of joint. They were on a stage away from the guys, with velvet curtains, special lighting and not expected to mingle with the guys. I still wasn't interested but I loved the music they danced to. It would be a fun way to spend the afternoon. After a while, they said: "Come on up, let us show you how to work a pole. It might come in handy one day, one-on-one." And that's all I'm going to say about that.

Hal finally found out where I was living and would pester me to go home with him. He was "sorry and didn't mean it." "It's not going to happen" I said. There are some things you spit out of your mouth that you can't put back in. Also, hitting me was not forgivable. One night, when I opened my door, it looked like a cyclone had swept through, then I realized all my clothes had been cut up and scattered all over the room. The law officers said it was a good thing I wasn't in there because he was in a killer's rage.

They called the MP's and I heard they threw him in the brig, took away a stripe, and he was ordered to pay me $1,000.00 for the loss of my clothes. He never did but the best thing was they banned him from the hotel and gorunds. I was making some headway. I thought that would be the end of Hal in my life. Not easy as that, he still had things he intended to do.

CHAPTER EIGHT
What Could Be Next

I had met a nice man that the bartenders had let in early so he could enjoy a couple of drinks in private. My new friend kept me company while I ate dinner. When I asked what his job was, he said he was one of the base chaplains. We had great conversations and I was thankful I once read a book titled "Religions of the World". One evening he asked me if I would like to have lunch at the officer's club the next day. I thought that sounded great; from strippers to chaplains. Was I having fun or what? When he picked me up the next day he said: "I have a buddy who is out getting some flight time in and he asked I would pick him up. I hope you don't mind if he joins us for lunch, because we are going to play golf later." The colonel's rank carried a lot of clout so we had a great spot to watch the plane come in.

Little did I know, my life was about to change again – Big Time! My prince charming didn't arrive on a white horse. He arrived flying a B-52. When he stepped out of the plane, we walked over and the colonel introduced us. When we touched hands, it was like an electric connection and I wondered did he feel what I felt. When he glanced at me, I knew he had. I knew and he knew we would be together forever. The world stood still until the colonel broke the spell. I wanted so much to say: "Where have you been? I've been through a lot looking for you." Love at first sight? You bet. I had a feeling inside of me like take a deep breath girl, relax, you just found the man who is going to love and take care of you and your son for the rest of your life.

The next evening, in walks Major James Hurn, the man of my dreams, with the chaplain. He started coming in every evening after work and one day on his way out, he said he had the next day off, would I spend it with me. "Are you kidding me??" He turned and said: "Call the bachelor officer's quarters if you change your mind." I replied: "Do not expect a call." After that, we saw each other when we could find time. He knew when I got up in the morning so he would order a breakfast tray sent up and then come over and have coffee with me. When he could find more time, we spent hours on deserted beaches, learning more about each other as we watched the hermit crabs and seagulls. One afternoon, we strolled through the poet Longfellow's gardens on one of our outings. We had lunch on the lawn from a basket the hotel made up for us.

The first evening I had off, he drove to a quaint little shack on a back bayou where many of the black sergeants and their dates hung out. We loved to sit back in the corner and watch them dance. A beautiful lady, called Lollipop, played piano like you couldn't believe. Every time we walked in, her next song was "Fascination" or "Strangers in the Night". At midnight, large bowls of crayfish gumbo were served. Then, we all tried to maneuver down a creaky old wooden walkway that crossed a swampy area full of alligators. The gators' eyes shine at night, so you could see lots of them. We were all like stuffed Thanksgiving turkeys with all that gumbo in us. I'm sure we would have been delicious. When we got to the car, I always looked back to see the lamp glow from the windows of this small magical place where we fell deeply in love. Later, I surprised him with a painting of the shack.

Hal had called Jim to meet him in a local hotel lobby. I asked: "Are you?" He said: "Yes." I asked what they talked about. He said: "He asked me to stop seeing you. My reply was that, it would be up to the lady wouldn't you think?" The next night, Hal, high on something, decided to kill himself. The couple living upstairs smelled gas and when they zoomed in on where it was coming from, they found Hal, unconscious, with the oven door open. They called the medics who came and took him to the base hospital. A chaplain was called in the next morning. Guess which one? Our old friend, the colonel, asked Hal what was so bad in his life that he would want to end it. Hal replied that an officer was trying to take his wife from him. I bet when he said: "Major Hurn", the colonel dropped his composure a bit, leaving very quickly to call his wayward friend and tell him what was going on. I received a call from Jim, saying the Colonel would be calling to tell me what had happened and to play it cool or he would be in deep trouble. I did get the call right away. He told me what Hal had done and what he said. He asked if Major Hurn was hitting on me; were we romantically involved? "You told me yourself, Colonel, I was a pretty southern belle, all the men hit on me, including Major Hurn. But, no, we aren't involved." (Lying to a chaplain didn't feel too good.) So then, he tried to talk me into counseling to work out our problems. After I told him what had gone on to make me reach the point of leaving; he said he understood why I wanted to forget I had ever known a Sergeant Greanhouse.

Jim called to say he wouldn't be in touch for a while but would see me as soon as he could. He also said, I don't think Greanhouse will bother you anymore. When I asked why he thought that, he said: "Because he's on his way to Minot, N.D." I now have a real man that will protect me at last. He offered to pay my way home, but I assured him that I had enough money. "See you soon, baby. Take care and know there's a man in Mississippi that's crazy about you." I couldn't get the grin off my face.

I knew a man had moved into the hotel recently that had an airplane he shared with his dad, who lived in Tampa. I was talking to him one night when he stopped in The Julep Room for a night-cap. He mentioned he was going home in a couple weeks to leave the plane with his folks. When I told him I was working to get back home to Orlando, he said I could hitch a ride if I wanted to. Of course, I did. I was so excited about seeing my child soon, and didn't have to buy a ticket. I had money saved up but had to spend it on new clothes when Hal destroyed what I had.

I thought I might be a member of the "mile high club" before we landed, but we had blue skies, smooth flying and good company with a perfect gentleman.

Jim and I did get to see each other once again before I left. We spent a week-end in New Orleans. I hadn't been there so I was very excited about it. We stayed in a hotel in the French Quarter and had dinner at the Court of Two Sisters, where a trio of violins stopped at our table and asked: "What would you two like for us to play for you this evening?" We were holding hands across the table and staring into each other's eyes. Jim slipped money to them and said: "You choose." The played: "Love is a Many Splendored Thing"; perfect as it gets. We were sad not knowing when we would see each other again. Any other special nights never lived up to this one.

CHAPTER NINE
Starting Life With Jim

I did get my job back, living with "I told you so" from the girls for several weeks. My answer was, just wait until you see what I found out there. I rented an apartment above another apartment so the carport or the lower one gave me a great place for grilling. A couple of lounge chairs and a few plants, made an inviting place to relax.

A D.J. that played romantic songs by request late at night always dedicated one to me. He loved the special cookies I brought him from the hotel.

Jim came to Florida several times that year. On one of those visits, he and two other officers stopped in the hotel lounge for a drink. They had attended a special meeting at Orlando Air Force Base. The three were in dress uniform, complete with medals, ribbons and thunder and lightning in their caps. If you've never seen this sight, I'm here to tell you, it will make you weak in the knees. The girls were flirting with them like crazy and when I told them: "That's what I found in Mississippi" Biloxi became a favorite vacation spot.

On the next visit, Jim told me he had been promoted to Lt. Colonel, and was being sent to Chicago to help man the recruiting headquarters for Illinois. He would be going off flying status, so I knew he wouldn't be dropping out of the sky at Orlando AFB anymore. I was happy for him, sad for me.

We were sitting on the deck after dinner listening to the radio. Aunt Vee was spending the week with me. She and Russ were rooting loudly for their favorite wrestler. We were laughing at them when I heard the D.J. say that he wasn't going to play a song for me that night. He was going to play a song requested by that sharp looking military officer he saw going into my apartment that afternoon. "So here you are Colonel, just for you. Here's Miss Ella with 'Unforgettable'." That's when he asked me if I would accept this ring which comes with the promise of marriage in the city of Chicago.

He would go back to Kessler, wrap up whatever he had to do, and be back in two weeks. He showed up in a Desoto station-wagon with his clothes and "Frederick Von-August" his beloved dachshund. It took us a couple of days to wrap up the things I needed to do. I couldn't do much before he came back because I wasn't exactly sure when that would be. I had packed a few boxes with pots and pans, blankets, pillows and of course, our clothes. Crazy, huh? What more does a couple need but love, a boy, and a dog?

The day before I left I called dad and said if he wanted to say good-bye to his grandson, he should come over because we were leaving the next morning. The step-monster would be with him, of course. I was trying to be nice, but this was a mistake. We were raked up one side and down the other for being so immoral as to live together, unmarried. He pointed that old crooked finger at me again and said in his special way, as he always did; "How did I raise you like I did and you turned out the way you did?" Jim got up and left the room and I Sat there laughing and wondering if his DNA ran through my veins. I asked them to leave.

I couldn't believe it. I had been married and divorced twice, had a six year old, and taken care of us without anyone's help what-so-ever. I was glad to be going far away from this place, where I had so much sadness. Don't count the evil witch out yet.

Aunt Vee was as happy as I was. She thought Jim hung the moon. I told her: "Of course he did." She told me she would marry him if I didn't. "It's a deal," he said. They would become great friend for the rest of their lives.

She wished us the best and gave us a beautiful afghan she had been working on for weeks. She left before dad and Dot arrived. When I snuggle with it every winter, I feel her hugging me and smiling. She and I had so many belly laughs together. We were thrilled when she came out to California to visit us. We took her from one end of the state to the other. I loved that lady with all my heart.

Aunt Vee didn't know we had a blow up with dad and Dot so Dot was able to get our address and phone number from her. That's when Dot sent me a letter saying that she was going to Jim's superior officer if she didn't get a marriage license soon. I couldn't believe this woman. Not knowing what she was capable of, we sent off a fake one. I refused all calls and sent mail back unopened. We would get married on our time and not hers. Will this woman ever leave me alone? No!

Even with all this, when they came near Chicago to attend a religious convention, they called saying quickly: "Don't hang up, someone you know has died. We would like to stop and visit." Are you kidding me? Along with all the things they had done to me, the fact that she would actually try and ruin Jim's career made me so mad. Then to think we would act like it was nothing. How stupid can you be? I had no contact with them for nine years.

Chicago was and still is one of the great cities. How exciting to be right in the middle of it, starting our life together. We arrived at an apartment that this boss had rented for us. He and his wife, Edna, lived there also.

We had picked up Chinese take-out and ate on an overturned cardboard box. Then we opened the same box, taking out sheets, blankets and pillows making a bed on the floor, where the four of us slept as tired and happy as we could be. We didn't care one bit about the inconvenience. We weren't in that apartment anyway, we were on cloud nine. The next morning we headed out to breakfast then furniture shopping. We also bought groceries and three sleeping bags. It would be several days before the furniture arrived. Russ got a kick out of having a dog. When Freddie snuggled with him in his sleeping bag instead of Jim's, he asked if he could call him, his dog.

Jim began his job the first week getting acquainted with staff then flew off to Texas to school for two weeks. The day after he arrived there, he sent me a dozen roses with a card saying: "I do promise you a rose garden." Jim loved growing roses, so our home always had vases full of them. We left many gardens of them behind. I have only one bush now, it being a "Chrysler Imperial" the name of the first one he gave me.

The furniture was slowly arriving, so I kept busy with that and getting my son settled into second grade. Winter was now upon us and having never seen a snowflake, we were anxiously awaiting the first snowfall. We hadn't shopped for winter clothes yet, so Freddie's walks were short ones. That wind off Lake Michigan was something to be reckoned with. Christmas was only a week away – no snow yet. All I wanted for Christmas was a white one. Jim said Santa would probably bring sleds and ice skates. When we went to bed on the 24th, the last thing we did was look outside; no snow. I was awakened by Jim in the middle of the night saying: "Look outside." I thought, how beautiful the falling snow was. It was more beautiful than I could have imagined. Russ and I couldn't wait to get outside. When we first stepped on the snow, we were surprised, thinking it would be like walking in marshmallow fluff, but we slipped and slid all the way down the steps. It was cold, slipper, hard and wet. We then went shopping for fur-lined caps that cover your ears, boots, gloves and heavy jackets.

On week-ends, we went to a nearby wooded park that had a shallow creek running through it where Jim taught us to ice-skate. What a thrill it was the first time we skated down the river with Russ between us. The beauty of the place was like being in a Courier and Ives painting. The animals were keeping warm in their dens, as were the people, so we usually had this wonderland to ourselves.

There was a shed with a fireplace and a box full of logs, so we always took wieners for roasting and marshmallows for toasting. Hot baked beans, hot cider and deviled eggs made a perfect winter picnic. I had always thought, if you had snow it would be cold, but if the wind isn't blowing, it can be quite nice.

There was a ranger who always stopped by when he saw smoke to check it out. He would say: "Oh, it's only you guys" then be on his way. We always offered him something to eat. One day he must have been hungry because he stayed and ate something and we made an interesting friend. It turned out he was an ex-military man, having been a navy seal, so he and Jim got a long like wild-fire. You can meet some interesting people along the way if you stop long enough to get passed Hello.

When spring arrived, Jim taught us to bowl, good enough to win trophies. That summer, he taught us what golf was all about, not good enough to win trophies. I never made it passed a three par course and was lucky to find some women who thought like I did, that it was all about fresh air and exercise.

So many wonderful new experiences; our lives were being lived to the fullest in a loving, positive way and we had only just begun. My life was the way I had always dreamed.

Freddie taught me to give my heart to a dog again. I have had the pleasure of their company ever since, usually several, plus a cat or two.

We began exploring the city on week-ends. One evening about dark, we got lost and found ourselves in the ghetto. It was Saturday night and the youth were restless. They surrounded the car, slowing us to a crawl, plus we were being pelted with something. Jim couldn't get a break to haul out of there. They were enjoying playing cat and mouse with us. After a bit, the leader stopped everyone and escorted us out. When I could speak, I said: "That was scary. Why would they do that?" Jim's reply was: "Got to get those Mississippi license plates off." It was 1962-63.

Jim would later open a recruiting office in that area, manned by two of his sharpest Sergeants. They had a blast of an opening day. There was lots of brass. Mayor Daly, celebrities, music and food. A good time was had by all. Those two recruiters never had a problem meeting their quota. They introduced their moms to the Air Force mother's club, making for good neighborhood religions. Jim said it only made sense to harness that energy. You had to have a high school grad to get into the Air Force so that was a plus because some of the ones that wanted to join had to finish first.

Chicago is a beautiful City with so much to offer. We explored every inch of it. The Museum of Science and Industry, being a favorite, as was the art museum. I discovered the department stores I had only heard of, Macy's, Carson P Scott and Marshall Fields. Their animated windows are unbelievable during the Christmas holidays. Everything was new and exciting to us. I'm sure Jim got a kick out of seeing it through our eyes.

During the week, I took cooking classes, learning three cuisines, preparing for the entertaining I knew was in my future. IT's funny today to hear Russ tell someone: "My mom used to know how to cook. She 'fondued, flambéed and souffled.'"

We visited Jim's family once a year. They had a cabin in the mountains where we would spend a few days. There was a shallow river flowing over rocks and pebbles with boulders large enough to sunbathe on. I was doing just that one day, when I looked up and saw Jim standing in the stream, dipping his hands into the water, coming up with double handfuls of pebbles, letting the water drip through his fingers. I asked "What are you doing, looking for gold?" He answered: "As a matter of fact, I am. I dropped my Masonic ring in here." After a few more tries, there it was in his hands. I couldn't believe it.

His parents were the kind I wished I had. Dad Hurn endeared himself to me the first time I visited their home by telling my little boy: "You and Freddie must be so tired of that back seat. Let's go out back and toss a ball."

If they dropped it, Freddie was right there to pick it up and run. After dinner, mom Hurn said: "Let's take a ride out to Washington's Crossing," Yep, that Washington, on the Delaware. I have a newspaper clipping of dad Hurn taking part in the yearly re-enactment.

I like his family very much. You would have thought I was his first wife, but they had been through this twice before.

Because of the good job of second in command in Chicago and his new rank, Jim was being transferred to California Civil Defense headquarters in Los Angeles as commander. They weren't meeting their quota, so new blood was needed. From one big city to another, I loved it. We wondered what awaited us there. Movie stars, for one thing, and we met quite a few.

Colonel Kramer and his wife, Edna, gave us a party in their penthouse. The view was awesome. I don't think a full colonel could have afforded it, but Edna could. She was a piece of work; a real glamour puss trying to imitate the Gabor sisters. She didn't want children because they would cramp her style; not to mention what they would do to her body. She pulled a few good ones on me. She told me an affair was formal when it was casual and visa-versa. I was glad we were leaving. After a cocktail party and everyone left, we headed out to dinner.

When we entered the elevator we joined two men dressed for a night on the toqn. They were very jovial and friendly with a head start on the night. When we got to the lobby, they shook hands and we all said to have a good time, and take a taxi home. They were dead tow minutes later. We all had headed for the door that the doorman was holding open when shots rang out. I guess the shooter got the ones he wanted. Our guys grabbed us and hit the floor, not really knowing what was happening.

The morning paper wrote of a mob hit. I kept the clipping for a long time. They were well known. We were very lucky that night. We went back up to their place and had scrambled eggs and Bloody Marys. It did seem the right time to get out of Dodge, do to speak. So California here we come.

CHAPTER TEN
Life in California

We had a month to relocate to the new assignment. Someone in the L.A. office was in charge of finding us a rental house. Not having that to worry about, we had a leisurely cross-country trip. I may not get to see much of the world but I sure was seeing a lot of the USA. If it was convenient, at the end of the day we stayed in the guest quarters on a military base. We enjoyed a break from fast food, having delicious dinners at the officers club. Because of the decal on Jim's car, he received a click of the heels and a sharp salute. If it was near 5PM, everything came to a halt until the flag was lowered.

Russ thought all this was pretty cool, so then and there, he declared he was going to be a soldier. As we headed west, it changed to cowboy. He had seen lots of cattle, but no cowboys yet. Of course, when he fell asleep, we saw lots of them. We used to tease the poor child relentlessly. By the way, it takes a loooong time to drive through Texas.

The person in charge of finding us a rental home did a good job. We had a great experience living in a Spanish villa that was perched above the town of Eagle Rock, California with the San Gabriel Mountains behind us. The state was going to put an off-ramp through that area so in the mean time you could rent one of these beautiful places. We found a note on the door that said: "Welcome to California". It certainly was looking good. I'll never forget our first Halloween there. I kid you not, at the bottom of a driveway gate; a butler with a cooler was handing out ice cream bars – and wipes. I can't resist, we aren't in Kansas anymore.

We checked out the neighborhood while walking Freddie. You could tell some of the houses were being pilfered. On a plaque cemented into a fountain at one of the houses, we saw the name: Tom Mix. He was a big cowboy star when Jim was growing up. We mentioned this and the butler at the gate to a neighbor. They told us an aging movie legend lived there but never left the house. I never found out who it was, but I do remember the butler asking the children to wave to the house.

The first week at the office, Colonel Hurn got acquainted with the facility and staff. They were located downtown in a huge building that was a constant hub of activity. Everything to do to prepare the men for "ship-out" was done there after the recruiters had done their job. There was testing, physicals, swearing in and sending them on their way to boot camp. You can imagine the enormous amount of paperwork this entailed. I suppose some of the enlisted spent the entire time in that building. The one and only time I visited, some nurses and doctors were being sworn in by a female captain who was a nurse herself. She was a recruiter for the medical inductees. God bless them all. It takes more than combat soldiers to man a military. The next week's schedule was for the boss to meet some of the recruiters, eventually meeting them all, as a few would come in each week. He was surprised at how rumpled and sweaty they looked; poster boys for the Air Force, they were not. They told him they had spent a lot of time in their cars which didn't have air-conditioning. The previous commander said it was against regulation. That, along with other problems, had taken the piss and vinegar out of them. A sergeant later told me his new boss had given the best pep talk ever. He stressed the importance of their job which greased the wheel that kept the whole machine working. It wasn't long before A/C was in all the cars, which picked up morale. They asked, wasn't he concerned about regulations? His answer was that some jokers think they have to go by the book to a ridiculous degree and he was quite sure the military had more important problems than to worry about A/C. You're the one that supplies that soldier, so we have to do that anyway we can so they can do their job.

By the way, some of the A/Cs came from a military warehouse in Sacramento that Jim new about. I assume he hit up local business owners for extras he needed.

Another change the Colonel made right away was to send the new recruits by air instead of Greyhound. "What do you mean, they aren't flying to boot camp? This is the Air Force," was heard loud and clear. Some of these young men may have never been on an airplane and may have jobs that have nothing to do with planes. It wasn't long before Continental Airlines was on the job. As a thank-you once a year, they took the boss, staff wives and girlfriend up for a flight over Catalina Island and then up and down the coast. We were served drinks and a box each of fabulous treats. We had a ball.

One of the big shots came to Jim's retirement party and had more fun that anyone. I have a priceless snapshot of him sitting in a sergeant's lap trying to kiss him.

We had several good Samaritans, one being a local business man I'll never forget. Saul Polk loved the military men and every Christmas he gave each family one of those large Santas that light up and you set on your lawn.

Another one was the brother of one of the office staff. He was visiting one day and met the colonel. He was the president of Seagram's and was visiting the local distributorship. From then on, every recruiter got a bottle of Seagram's best for their birthday. The president said no one had ever asked him before. This was good publicity. What do you think the guys bought when they went to the liquor store? Later on, I remember the Colonel being asked to do a favor for his son who was enlisting in the Air Force. Payback time. Jim must have pulled some strings, because from then on until Jim left each wife received a velvet box with Champagne and two flutes on their anniversary.

The recruiters loved their new boss and worked hard to show it. Oh, I also loved their boss a lot. It wasn't long before they were raising the numbers in all the detachments. He was there two years.

The Rose Parade was coming up soon. We were excited because Eagle Rock was near Pasadena. The recruiter from the office got us back stage passes, so they let us fill water vials that held the flowers. People camped on the sidewalks days ahead, so policemen were everywhere and the town was lit up like Times Square. The workers on the floats would be busy all night, they said. A part atmosphere prevailed and we stayed until midnight and watched the parade on TV the next day. We would go to the game later with some UCLA alum because the Trojans were playing. My first ever football game, such harmless fun, how could that have been a sinful thing to attend back when I was in high school?

Public relations were in full swing in the LA area. The recruiters were doing a great job. It wasn't long before we were visiting movie sets. A fun story involved "No Time for Sergeants" a big TV hit at that time. Coming off break to do the next scene, they took Russ into the cockpit with them. The director appears and yells, "Quiet on the set, roll 'em, take one." A minute later he's yelling: "Cut, where in the hell is that script girl when I need her?" She comes running and he's jabbing at the paper saying: "Where on here does it say there's red-headed boy in this scene?" She was as surprised as he was. The stars are cracking up. The director is mad as a hornet and Russ missed his one shot at being a TV star. Good thing it was a hit show, retakes are costly, I am told. The director said: "If you bunch of no-good airheads are through horsing around, we can wrap and go home."

There was another set filming Highway Patrol with Broderick Crawford who was the star. He fit the role well, being a big, rough, tough looking man. Jim and Russ had gone into a restroom when in he walks, unzips next to them and looks down at Russ and said: "I've got the worst bastard for a director I've ever had. How's yours kid?" Jim and Russ didn't miss a beat, he told him: "He wasn't very nice, he just told me to get my ass off his set."

As Crawford left, he said: "Bring your boy over to my set if you have time and don't let it get you down kid. One day you'll be a star." The 'kid' was very excited because he never missed an episode of Highway Patrol.

Bonanza was another hit at the time. They let us on their set anytime and would visit with us when on break. Very nice guys.

Before we left any set, pictures were taken as the Colonel presented beautiful large model airplanes with a brass plaque that read: I support the USAF. Pictures usually showed up in the next day's newspaper.

The farewells at the airport to see Bob Hope and his gang off on another USO tour were always a thrill. Great PR for both the stars and the military because the pictures showed up in newspapers and on TV. The Colonel had his own photographer who was always around. Bob Hope was so funny. The man is "on" all the time. The world was indeed his stage. He was a true American treasure. I have priceless photo of Jim looking every bit the military officer but his photographer snapped him just as he was sneaking a peak at Carol Baker. She was a very sexy, popular actress, wearing a flimsy dress with no bra. The chilly day made her nipples erect. Guess where the colonel's eyes were. He asked them to tear it up but at his retirement party he was given an album of those two years in pictures. That one was among them. He was a good sport because they had fun with it in the office before they put it in hiding.

The laughter had hardly died down, when one morning Jim said he didn't have any clean shorts, only the ones I have him for Valentine's Day with the red hearts. I felt bad being a new wife. I said I was sorry but no one was going to see his shorts, I hoped! Wrong! The office was always a bee-hive of activity but when it was time to square in the new recruits who were heading to boot camp, the Colonel had to stop what he was doing and run downstairs to swear them in. He thought that's what it was. When he arrived, the doctor said to him: "It's time for you yearly vaccinations and I'm caught up so drop your pants and take it like a man." He did, having forgotten about the shorts. The room burst out laughing. I was so glad the photographer wasn't there. The doc called me and said to chill Martinis and cook his favorite meal. It wasn't fun around my house for several days. I hadn't seen the Colonel mad before. It's not a pretty sight. Later on we had some laughs about it. At his retirement party, one of the sergeants wore them in a "This is your life" skit. I was surprised I still had them but it was a hit of the skit.

While in LA, one evening stands out above all others. We were invited to the world premiere of "Sand Pebbles". To our surprise, the car ahead of us stopped at the red carpet and out stepped Elizabeth Taylor, the star of the movie, and Richard Burton. Steve McQueen, the male start, was also attended but we didn't see him. We got to walk the Red Carpet behind them and I can tell you, she was so beautiful it hurt your eyes to look at her. Mr. Burton had a pot-marked face but it didn't take away from his manly looks. Masculinity oozed from every pore. Some of the fans could reach my clothing and tugged at me asking: "Who are you? I don't recognize you." I wanted to say: "Just a little girl from a cotton field in Alabama who held onto dreams of a better life with a partner who would hug instead of hit and have a ball along the on life's red carpet."

We went to a party afterwards with the stars, including quite a few legends. Too many to mention, but I can tell you, Edward G. Robinson made me do a double take. I don't know why it's suck fun to see them in person. They don't seem real somehow until you do. From the screen to standing next to you, complementing your gown is a kick. It really is fun to meet a favorite and get to talk with them. No show biz talk, I was told. It certainly took all the composure I could muster to keep from gaping when John Wayne walked up and shook Jim's hand. We got an invite to Newport Beach to a party the next weekend. His yacht was parked there, a converted PT boat we were told. He had friends living in Newport Beach at the time and we spent the night with them.

All this hardly seemed real, I was Cinderella finally out of the wicked step-mother's reach and I got to go home and sleep with my Prince Charming. Oh, did I tell you? He was as handsome as any movie star. I am a lucky girl. But if he had mistreated me, I would have moved on.

Jim had actually spent time in Hollywood before. After the war, he flew reconnaissance on the Russian border and re-mapping flights. He was assigned to be Edward R. Murrow's pilot for a few weeks when the news man was doing a documentary. At one point he was in charge of a warehouse full of camera equipment. I would guess knowledge of film got on his records because when he was back in the states he was given a large budget to hire producers to make recruiting films which were shown in movie theaters before the main film started. I guess that's where recruiting go ton a his record. I don't know if Hal Roach made any of these but he spoke of him with high regard.

I haven't yet written about his war experiences. I remember a few years ago, the old War Birds flew into Leasburg. Jim showed me an airplane like the one he spent many hours crammed into the cockpit and quite a few sitting on the ground leaning against a wheel, sleeping. Of all the pictures I have, that's my favorite. It was a fun day for us.

When Jim was a Captain, he went to the university in Norman, Oklahoma to get his B.A. After that he was sent to Newfoundland as a squadron adjunct for four years. When he was promoted to major he was sent to Keesler Air Force Base in Biloxi, Mississippi as the base adjunct. He was still beefing up his flight status. I don't know how long he had this position when I came along and turned his world upside down.

We spent two years in California before he decided to retire to after twenty-two years in the military. He wrestled with this because once you're this close to your first star it's difficult to hand it up. I kept quiet on this decision. Either way was fine.

I'm not going to write anymore about his retirement party except to say the staff went all out and it was a blast. It was obvious that he was well liked. They gave him a wooden airplane propeller with a brass plaque that had his name, rank and detachment emblem on it. Mom Hurn still had hs cadet book which he was surprised to see. I saw the picture of the graduating class and underneath his photo it said: "The most eager of them all." That's my guy!

CHAPTER ELEVEN
Civilian Life

Jim was anxious to get out into the real world. He got a job with the city of Anaheim as assistant civil defense director. He had bought our first home there. Disneyland was new. Tourists were everywhere. The town was booming. New businesses were opening every day. We adjusted to civilian life very well. Jim was busy with his new job so I busied myself putting our home in order. It was so beautiful. I couldn't believe it was actually ours. It had a sunken swimming pool with a fountain of a small boy peeing in the water. Large urns on each corner held topiaries. It was a great house for entertaining and that we did.

Jim immediately put in our first rose garden and built Russ a tree house. Life was good; vases full of roses, a beef roast baking in the oven and martinis chilling in the fridge.

I became vice-president of the PTA and did substitute teaching when needed. We both got very active in politics. Ronald Reagan was running for governor of California at this time. We beat the bushes up and down the state for him. Eddie Arnold came out from Nashville to help draw crowds. We were in his group, nice man, such a gentleman. When he stepped off the plane, the crowds went wild. Other celebs joined us off and on. When Reagan won he threw a celebration party in Hollywood for some of his supporters. As you know, he went on to become our 40th president.

Jim joined several civic clubs and played golf once a week. He was asked to join a group of businessmen called, "The Ambassadors". Their duty was to show up in top-hat and tails with the mayor and Miss Anaheim to cut the ribbon at new business openings. There was always a lavish buffet and drinks, so most were held after five o' clock. Hotels were sprouting up all around Disneyland along with restaurants, gift shops, etc.

I remember saying to the girls one day when we were hanging out by the pool and due to attend one of those openings in a couple hours that I thought I might go to AA. "I think I'm beginning to drink too much." The Orange County gals replied: "Nonsense dahling, we all do, don't worry."

We had a lot of house guests while we lived there. I'm not sure it was us they wanted to see. Instead of "Hurn House" I think it was the "Mouse House" they were interested in.

Our very first year my sister, Carol, husband Jerry and their two children drove out so the kids could see some of the U.S. and SUR-PRISE! – dad.

Dot had died the year before, I had been bombarded by phone calls and letters from her family begging me to please come for a short visit so she could see Russ once more and she wanted to tell me something important. They didn't know how she had treated me. I finally caved in, knowing there were others I could visit. She was thrilled to see Russ but we had left Florida when he was six and this was 9 years later. As a 15 year old teenager, he was very nonchalant. As for me, she begged forgiveness. I don't believe you can raise hell all your life, then say oops, sorry about that and expect the person to say: "That's alright, it was nothing." So, you'll have to guess which way I went. She could talk to her god about forgiveness.

Dad said he never realized just how far Florida was from California and said he thought they never would get through Texas. He said he wished he could tie that Chevy on the tail of a jet to get home. He liked the house and the pool, saying we must be doing well. He could tell there was happiness there because of the warm, loving atmosphere.

Somehow, Russ had fond memories of Paw Paw so he spent some time with him. All I could think was: "What a wasted life." Once I asked him if he was sorry he and my mother didn't work things out, he said no.

Back to my houseguests. One night dad mentioned there was a lot of traffic from the backyard to the tree house today. I would check later on to find the wall papered with playboy bunnies. Uncle Jerry claimed it for his bedroom. Jim smoothed my feathers to say it was natural for teenage boys to be interested in forbidden magazines.

Everyone loved Disneyland and Knotts Berry Farm. We were less than five miles away, so we enjoyed the fireworks each night while we took a swim before bedtime.

The sons-in-law decided to take their father-in-law out on the town one night. We asked later where they had taken him. He said the rascals had twisted his arm and lef him astray to one of those tittie bars that had sprung up everywhere. The guys said: "Are you kidding? We pulled him out of there, kicking and screaming. The Rev. loved it, even had a couple shots of Wild Turkey." I was glad to see he was human after all and wondered if he thought he had lead too strict a lifestyle.

We all went to a theater-in-the-round one night. They were very popular at the time with dinner and a show. It was quite raunchy but funny. A friend was starring in ti and he said he heard "Brother Miller" as he called him, above everyone else laughing. I think "Brother Miller" wished he hadn't been so straight laced after all.

Jerry was a professional painter for the Holiday Inns. He told us to buy paint and supplies and he would paint our house before they left. Jim always said it took ten gallons of paint and five gallons of Bourbon. He and Carol did eventually divorce because of h is drinking and womanizing, making up her mind one night when she called and a woman answered.

She was single ten years before she remarried. She was manager of the Clermont Elks Club and later married the treasurer.

She died at sixty-two of a stroke. I was so shocked because we had just talked and she had planned on coming over to spend the night. She was finishing up the breakfast dishes when she called for her husband in the backyard. The EMTs were only three blocks away and got there very quickly. Her heart stopped for nine minutes. They sat outside the house trying to revive her. At the hospital, she was pronounced brain dead. She had a living will. IT's so hard to say good-bye to someone who had been a part of your life from the beginning. She had always told me she was tied to my apron strings and I better no try to get away. She did visit us everywhere we lived. My brother-in-law comes over and takes me out to a nice restaurant once in a while. He's a friend to me. He went back to work at seventy because, he said, it wasn't much fun watching grass grow. He lives about an hour away as does my son and daughter-in-law.

My sister, Gail lives about an hour away. She had three children by her first husband and one by her second. They were married five years when he was killed in a most tragic way. He worked for the road department and Gail had dropped him off at his work spot for the day and was to be back at 5PM to pick him up. When she arrived on time, he saw her and flashed his hand to indicate ten minutes. The workmen were spreading the hot tar and gravel as it was pouring off the truck. When this last load was raised to empty, the dump truck cable broke and he was covered in the stuff. She became a recluse. I hope to spend some time with her now that I live nearby.

My sister, Carol, daughter-in-law, Betty and myself opened an antique shop, taking turns, two days each a week. We loved it but I got out rather quickly deciding to work at an assisted living on the three to eleven shifts. I would then know for sure how much I would make each week. You don't just stand behind the counter and take the money in an antique shop. You're out there hustling all the time. You aren't in the store. We were going into Orlando for auctions, estate sales, and people's homes who want to sell you something. The newness of it all became old fast.

CHAPTER TWELVE
Changing Times and Places

The drugs were flowing into Orange County from Mexico and parents panicked after two teens died in our neighborhood. The boy next door hung himself and the other boy was found dead in the backseat of his car. He lived a few blocks away. Both were friends of our family. Parents started placing their children in boarding schools, Jesuit schools and military academies. We realized one night when Russ came in that he had glassy eyes and he was going to the hospital to have his stomach pumped if he didn't fess up. He did and we went to the source to check it out. The friend he had gotten the pills from was being drilled by his parents. We took Russ to visit a military academy to see if he would be interested in attending school there. He didn't want to do that. We had lived in Anaheim, eight years by now and had grown tired of the lifestyle. Jim and I discussed the idea of a complete change by moving farther north to the San Joaquin Valley, called the "bread basket of the nation" because of the wide variety of produce grown there and the amount. We actually export rice which surprised me. We had driven through there on our way to San Francisco several times.

Not only did we want change, when we discussed this plan with Russ, he was excited to go where he could enjoy all that a rural setting offered; hunting, fishing, etc.

Jim sent off resumes to several counties in that area. Two responded and he went up for an interview. He nailed them both, choosing

Merced County because there was an Air Force Base there. He was the new Civil Defense director. The job was a breeze for him so when an opening for fleet manager came along, they offered it to him also with a raise and two secretaries to help him do the job. He later became the president of the Northern California Civil Defense. He would later go to DC to speak before congress about the readiness of that area.

We lived of forty acres, twenty miles from Merced. We were right miles from Los Banos (The Baths), so named by the padres who had established missions up and down California. It is a Portuguese and Italian town, wonderful people. We were adopted by a family who were a mix of both. The included us into their life like one of their own.

When Jim went to DC, we asked a couple who were our best friends to go with us. We also called Jim's daughter who lived in NC and asked if she and hubby would meet us there. They did and we went sight-seeing while Jim was in meetings.

We enjoyed his daughter and son-in-law for a couple of days; roaming around Georgetown and a tour of the Whitehouse. They had to get back to their jobs so our time together was short. That night we hired a limo to pick us up the next morning to take us on a tour of all the monuments. When we finished the tours, we still had two hours so the driver suggested we go to Mt. Vernon. All in all, it was a fantastic day. That night over dinner we decided to check out that zoo to see the panda the next day.

The next morning my friends needed film. We saw a drugstore down a side street and headed there. It was cold and windy and early so the side streets were empty at the moment. However, there was an old wine-o leaning against the wall. I didn't need film so I told them I would keep him company. I said: "Good morning" and he did also. I told him I would give him money for a heavier coat if he wouldn't buy wine with it. He said, "Thank you ma'am, your sure are nice, but I can't promise." He said he could tell we were tourists and wouldn't it be a kick to see the president while you're here. I said I would be over-joyed to add a photo of him into my DC album. We were silent for a while then he pointed to the roof of a hotel and asked if I see those men on the top with rifles. "Yes, but what's going on? Why the rifles?" That's because President Carter is in there talking to the Olympic winners. He will be going right by here anytime because he's been there quite a while.

Frank and Dolores came out and I told them what the wine-o said. Frank said: "What the hell does he know? Even if he's right, we could stand here for an hour." About that time, here comes the president's motorcade; motorcycles, two more cars with secret service, then the president's car with his flag on one fender and the US flag on the other. He put the window down and waved at us. Behind that a couple more motorcycles and one last car that stopped in front of us. The "wine-o" jumped in as he waved and said, "Have a nice day in DC."

Back to Los Banos; Russ was graduating that year and decided to join the army. He did boot camp at Fort Ord in Monterey, then special training at Fort Bliss in Texas. He was home for two weeks then off to Germany for two years. The day he stepped into that plane in San Francisco, it hit me that baby bird had flown the nest and momma bird was crying her eyes out. Now I could identify with military moms.

The day we put Russ on the airplane he made reservations at my favorite hotel in Chinatown because I liked nothing better than running around there and ducking into some little dive and eating noodles.

So when he called me one day from work and said: "I have a surprise for you if you can get here in thirty minutes." I knew it must be something extra special. I was to meet him at the entrance gate to the base. I did. He said, slide over, then headed to an airstrip. There were about twenty people standing around. I mentioned the lack of airplanes. He said: "There comes one in now." I was dumbfounded, but he wasn't about to tell me anything. I noticed an American flag on a tailfin and what looked like a Presidential seal on the plane. Now I know, I'm going to see the President of the United States of America, but it wasn't. Then whoever was in charge, lines us up, giving us British flags and told us to hold them in our left hand because you'll need the right one to shake hands. When the door to the plane opened there stood The Queen of England, waving, Prince Philip was behind her. She opted not to shake hands but nodded her head and we did get a snapshot. I was awestruck because I do have a passion for English history. I couldn't get the smile off my face for a week. They both loved Yosemite so before going home they were going to spend some time at a lodge there. A caravan was waiting and off they went. The Britannia was docked in San Francisco Bay, waiting to take them back to England. A sad ending to their trip was the loss of three of their agents in a car accident on the winding mountain road.

I told Jim: "You can stop now with the surprises, because you can't top that." He said: "Since I couldn't take you to see her, I had to bring her here to see you.

While in Los Banos, I got two years of college under my belt, plus a cram course in nursing. I also picked up my artwork again, becoming a prize-winning sculptor after five year of study.

We had been living in the country for thirteen years by now and often spoke of moving back east so Jim could be closer to his daughter.

We lacked a washer and dryer so I had to go to town to do my laundry then grocery shopping. I could get all the clothes cleaned in an hour and a half. At home I seemed to have a pile of dirt laundry all the time. One day after I had taken the clothes inside from the car, I popped the trunk and went back to get the good stuff. I saw a pair of white silk panties laying the driveway. I thought how odd I hadn't seen them when I pulled them in, thinking I had dropped them when I put the basket in before I left. But, they were clean, so I guessed somehow I had just overlooked them. I dismissed it, but I found another pair a few days later and I hadn't gone to the laundry mat. But, we had a family visiting us that had two daughters and a mom. So, I thought when they were packing the car – but somehow I wasn't sure. Because I didn't know what to think, I again, dismissed it. Later I found a pair on my door that had been ejaculated into. I was red hot mad and scared. IT all made sense now. Thinking whoever was doing this could be inside I quickly left and went to a neighbor's house. We called the police and the investigators checked out the new facility that had been built on the property to house the workers, and found nothing. But, when they checked out the old place that was boarded up they found 200 pairs if panties. They concluded it was one of the men that worked there. That sped up our plans to leave. So, Jim turned in his resignation and we called the moving van.

We flew into Philly, rented a car, stopped for a couple days at mom and dad Hurn's. After that, we headed south, stopping along the way to visit Jim's daughter, Linda, and her family in Lincolnton, about 30 miles north of Charlotte. It's a beautiful town (area) and we fell in love with it. Halfway between Pennsylvania and Florida was perfect.

The place we bought was a beautiful two story, two acres with pink and white dogwoods and many wildflowers, plus a stream. By now we had two German Shepherds, Duke and Tasha. They loved the little stream and if one got in the water the other one would run along the side and wouldn't let him out. I made trails and planted an herb garden plus hundred of daffodils. Jim had a huge vegetable garden where he would spend countless hours.

I got a job as assistant director of activities at a 200 bed facility. I enjoyed it for three years. We had bought a beautiful two story brick home with a brook running through the property. I was anxious to make it a true southern garden, so I quit my job and took a master gardening course. I got a job at a local nursery working for free plants for our place. Customers began to ask me to speak at their garden clubs. That led to planting gardens, jazzing up the gardens they already had and eventually, with two young men helping, we put in complete landscaping at a lot of entrances to housing developments, islands in new shopping areas, etc.

All this led to me being asked to do one of the three gardens at a designer house. There was an evening stroll garden, a water garden, and I did the entrance that led to a circular drive. This was donated work but work offers poured in because we were allowed to place discreet small signs in our gardens.

When a garden tour went through our own garden, a Kuwaiti couple flipped out over the place. They called that night and asked if we would be at all interested in selling. We had wanted to buy near water, so I asked Jim, what would be the asking price if we sold it. He told me, and I tacked $25,000 on to that and they bought it – *cash*. We were there for eight years and did enjoy getting to know his daughter and her family better. Jim got his real estate license and he and Linda had offices in the same building for a while. She has two boys and one of them has given her two grandchildren. She and I have a good relationship. I think she is one of the sweetest people I ever met and a great mom.

We then bought a lovely place in Alabama on a lake. As is my style, I planted flower beds and painted and made the place beautiful. We had a large iron gate at the entrance to welcome you. Russ had brought it out and he and Jim installed it. I enjoyed taking to the lake in my paddle boat with me dogs along for the ride. Our home was in a small lakefront development a few miles outside of Birmingham. We had only been in the new place for two years when Jim tried to get out of bed one morning and fell back twice. He had carotid artery disease and wasn't doing well saying he didn't feel like he was going to make it. He wanted to get me closer to my family in Florida.

CHAPTER THIRTEEN
Back to Florida

We bought a place in the charming town of Mt. Dora. It was full of antique shops, outdoor cafes, pubs, etc. Tourists love it. So did we. There are 10 or 12 Bed and Breakfast and Inns. They swarmed with locals and tourists alike the year long.

Jim began to improve but all he wanted to do was read in his recliner, take the dogs to the park and socialize a little. My closest girl-friend's husband was a full Colonel so that worked out well. The two of them became great friends, and we've shared good times together.

My sister, Carol, daughter-in-law, Betty and myself opened an antique shop, taking turns, two days each a week. We loved it but I got out rather quickly deciding to work at an assisted living on the three to eleven shifts. I would then know for sure how much I would make each week. You don't just stand behind the counter and take the money in an antique shop. You're out there hustling all the time you aren't in the store; going into Orlando for auctions, estate sales, and people's homes who want to sell you something.

CHAPTER FOURTEEN
Losing Jim

Jim lived another twelve years but continued to go downhill. He got cancer of the prostate. Then he was diagnosed with emphysema and had to have oxygen 24/7. Then he had to have heart surgery. He became more incapacitated. On one of the hospital stays, he had to go to a rehabilitation nursing home because he was losing strength in his legs. He was then diagnosed with necrotizing fasciitis, the flesh eating bacteria. He was operated on and had to transfer to Orlando because they have in-house hyperbaric chambers which he needed. Then he had the skin removed from the back of his upper legs to graft the front. One dang thing after another, going from a walker to a wheelchair then bedridden for four years. I was so glad I had just enough experience to take care of him at home.

I felt I needed to prepare myself so we sold the house we were in and bought a place in one of the many "over fifty-five" communities here in Florida. I have a covered pool near the bank of the river where you can catch bass, catfish and tilapia. I have a boat docked out back that friends like to go out in because it takes you out to the lake.

Jim loved watching the fishermen and the pool activity. He was here for three years.

The night before he died, I got up to check on him. I was wearing an old sating sleep shirt and has one boob missing from a mastectomy three years earlier, I was startled when he whistled at me and said: "For an old broad, you're still pretty." I told him: "You don't have your glasses on. Seventy year old women aren't very pretty." He said: "Mine is." I smiled at him and kissed his cheek and said: "We certainly were a pair. How lucky can you get?" He said: "Pretty damn lucky." He said he was sorry he was putting me through this. I hugged and kissed him and said: "It could be the other way around and since you've been a good father, great husband and fantastic lover it is my pleasure to take care of you. Now goodnight, see you in the morning."

The next morning I gave him his V-8 juice as usual and went out to get his newspaper saying: "I'll be right back." "I'll be right here," he said. When I came back in, I thought he was asleep at first, but something made me take a closer look. He had slipped away.

The grief you feel makes you wonder how your heart keeps beating.

I feel so grateful to have found the love of my life to share such an interesting, exciting forty-six years. I try not to be sad because his worn out body is no longer confined to a hospital bed. I do want to say, he handled it like the real man he was.

It has been eighteen months now. So glad I made lasting friends along the way. I've received lots of cards and letters, the most touching being the ones from their children saying how much we meant to them. Several girlfriends have come to stay awhile. Love them for that and also for the steady support of family members. What a journey this has been, from the limb of a grapefruit tree to my life with my prince charming.

The End

Jim and his "Working girls"

Southern Belle Antiquities
The Mullberry Room

TINA HURN
(352) 735-6416 Bus.
(352) 383-1625 Res.

402 N. Fourth Avenue
Mount Dora, FL 32757

SEQUOIA NATIONAL PARK

GENERAL SHERMAN

YOSEMITE
NATIONAL PARK

YOSEMITE
WAWONA TREE

DREA DeMATTEO AND SHOOTER JENNINGS FOR AVERY BOARDMAN

Olean & her sisters
& Carol & Tina
gail came later

Mom
Olean

Papa's first wife
Olean Nelson

Tina & Carol in
a sweet potato
patch

Grand pa Miller
with Carol &
Tina gail

. See
the
look
A like
dresses
Olean
made

if ?
pressing
little thing
huh ?

H. F. M. LATER
TINA HURN

RUSS HURNS'
Mother
TINA

el tou this
missed up her
mouth

2 COUSINS of
TINA HURN

PAPA's parents &
your Mother at
4 yrs of Age

2 people I
never loved
Fredericksburg Drug Store

TINA CAROL and
GAIL.

T. A. Miller
with TINA, CAROL
& GAIL

This is where I play with the Pontoon

Love from Florida

Greetings from EUSTIS

Eustie, I went Nuts at XMAS withe Decor

Den ↓

Kitchen overlooking the pool ↓ Living room

D.C. trip (dinner)

NOTE:
Tony C. &
Alan C

VISITOR'S PASS

U.S. House of Representatives

WASHINGTON D.C.

Mrs Jim Hurn
for the Ninety-sixth Congress

Tony Coelho M.C.

D- 96708

Please see reverse side for Rules of the Gallery

Banquet here

United States Senate Chamber

Admit Washington D.C. Feb 26 1979

Mrs Jim Hurn

To the visitors gallery

For 96TH CONGRESS 1ST SESSION

Alan Cranston

U.S. SENATE

U.S. CIVIL DEFENSE COUNCIL

**Congressional Reception
and Dinner**

FEBRUARY 26   6:30 P.M.

Blue Room

United States Senate Chamber

Admit Washington, D.C. Feb 26 1979

Mrs Jim Hurn

To the visitors gallery

For 96TH CONGRESS 1ST SESSION

Alan Cranston

U.S. SENATOR

U.S. CIVIL DEFENSE COUNCIL

Congressional Reception
and Dinner

FEBRUARY 26   6:30 P.M.

Blue Room

HURN, JAMES L.
Lt Colonel, 17294A
17 September 1965

I'm seeing
Star's Jim's Boss
Here in

2 y the T.V. Stars from
BONANZA P.R. for
AND miss Calif. AF.

T.V. Show   P.R. for
STARS }   A.F.
"No Time for Sgt."

Tina & Carol in
a sweet potato
patch

Olean, Tina, Carol

your grand
Mother →

my Mother's father —
my grandfather
your great grandfather

my dads father, my grandfather + your great grandfth

Alabama

me

TINA & CAROL) the old farm house

WATER
MARK

Wendy Lawrence - STS-67, 86, 91, and 114

going out To A Party

Tina

We've been together

a long time now.

We've laughed and cried

and seen each other through

our best and worst

and everything in between.

And today, when I look at you,

I feel even more love

than I've ever felt before.

We have a history together,

full of shared memories

that keep us close.

You are so much a part of me

and a part of my happiness

that it's impossible to imagine

what life would have been like without you.

You are my partner

and my love,

and I ask nothing more

than to spend all the rest

of my life with you.

Linda Lee Elrod

PHOTOS BY HEIDINES PEREZ / DAILY COMMERCIAL

Visitors watch the B-17G Flying Fortress aircraft at the Wings of Freedom display on Saturday at the Leesburg Airport. The B-17G is one of the iconic bombers of WWII.

Wings of Freedom

MILLARD K. IVES | Staff Writer
millardives@dailycommercial.com

Pilot Steven Strong of Leesburg has flown plenty of smooth rides but on Saturday morning his flight was much different.

Strapped into the seat of a North American TP-51C Mustang warplane, accompanied by a primary pilot, he sped down a runway at the Leesburg International Airport and climbed into the sky where he was able to perform barrel rolls and other stomach-turning maneuvers.

"It was incredible," said Strong, who was awarded the trip as a birthday present.

The Mustang and two other iconic aircraft from World War II are on dis-

play this weekend at the airport where residents can reminisce as part of the Collings Foundation's annual Wings of Freedom Tour. It continues today at the airport and patrons can sign up for the Mustang flight as long as they're willing to part with the $2,200 fee for a half hour "excursion" or $3,200 for a full hour.

The tour honors veterans of WWII and America's other wars.

Korean War veteran John Carollo took time to explore the Boeing B-17 Flying Fortress "Nine O Nine," one of the most widely recognized WWII aircraft. The heavy bomber is powered by four 1,200-horsepower engines and has a wingspan of more than 103 feet.

SEE WINGS | A4

The brown-and-light green colored plane brought back memories for Carollo who once worked as an air traffic controller.

"I think every man should be made to serve at least two years in the military," said Carollo, standing by the plane's bomb bay opening.

The B-17 on display has three swastikas pasted on its side, denoting the number of German planes it shot down. It also boasted 140 miniature "bombs," representing the number of missions it flew.

Also on display was the Consolidated B-24J Liberator "Witchcraft," a four-engine bomber measuring 67 feet in length, and the only plane of its kind flying today, according to the foundation.

With a red nose and red stripes on its tail, it has 11 swastikas affixed to one side.

Touring the inside of the plane required a fair amount of agility. Determined visitors climbed up a ladder to enter the plane, maneuver their way across a walking plank and squeezing past radios, gun torrents, oxygen tanks, machines guns and an old "no smoking in the bomb bay" sign to get a good look at the cockpit.

But the sights inside were worth the effort, said Mike Hennessey, after crawling through the Liberator.

"I've seen a lot of warplanes on television and in the movies but seeing them up close is all together different," Hennessey said.

Admission is $12 for adults and $6 for children. The event is free for WWII veterans.

LEFT: People lline up for a look inside the B-17G. RIGHT: The gift shop provided pictures and accounts of the WW II air war.

(handwritten margin note) the plane Jim flew in WWII → I suprised Russ with a flight they let him sit in the Bomb

SAN LUIS RESERVOIR O'Neill Forebay

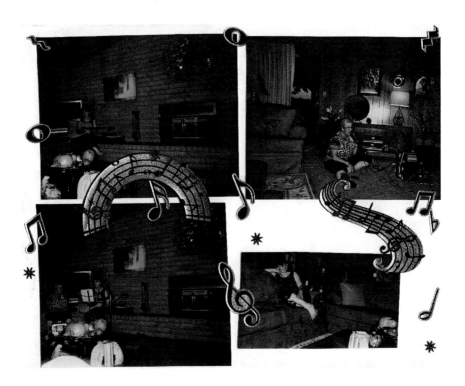

NAPA VALLEY

A friend from Napa visited

Hadn't seen Julliann more than
30 yrs. It was like yesterday